ADULT WAY

Mowbray Parish Handbooks

ADULT WAY TO FAITH

A PRACTICAL HANDBOOK WITH RESOURCES TO PHOTOCOPY

Peter Ball

MOWBRAY

Mowbray
A Cassell imprint
Villiers House, 41–47 Strand, London WC2N 5JE, England
387 Park Avenue South, New York, NY 10016–8810, USA

The services following Worksheet 8A are reproduced by kind permission of the various authors (see pp. 88–94, 96–101 for details).

First published 1992

British Library Cataloguing-in-Publication Data
A catalogue record for this book is available from the British Library.

Library of Congress Cataloging-in-Publication Data
Available from the Library of Congress.

ISBN 0-264-67267-4

Typeset by Colset Private Limited, Singapore
Printed and bound in Great Britain by Biddles Ltd,
Guildford and King's Lynn

Contents

Preface

A great many people have helped me in the writing of this book. Mostly they are people who share with me an enthusiasm for the Adult Way to Faith as a means of accompanying adults on their journey to Christian commitment and church membership. We see this approach as one that combines a number of important aspects of contemporary church life. It offers a method of evangelization; it recognizes the centrality of a ministry for every member of a congregation; it emphasizes the importance of a powerful liturgy which is both rooted in the spiritual tradition of the community and expressive of individuals' own lives.

First I thank Angela, my wife, not only for the support that she has given me in parish and cathedral ministry over the years of our marriage, but here especially for the particular way she has helped this book with her many readings of the typescript and creative suggestions.

I also wish to express my gratitude to colleagues in the Catechumenate Network, for help given in the years we have worked together. In particular, Malcolm Grundy and Sandy Hayter have been part of the making of this book. I also express my thanks to long-standing friends and colleagues on the European Conference on the Catechumenate, as well as to many Roman Catholics and Episcopalians with whom I have worked in North America and from whom I have learnt much. Those who know them will recognize how much I owe to succeeding generations of leaders in the French Catechumenate, in particular to Henri Bourgeois and the Lyon team, and to Jim Dunning and the people who work in the North American Forum on the Catechumenate.

None of this would have been possible without the people who started it all for me: those at St Nicholas, Shepperton. Confirmation candidates, the friends who accompanied them in preparation groups and their leaders, have all contributed to the following pages. So too have countless others from various parishes whose stories lie behind what I have written.

I am very grateful to Nancy Hammond for her interest in the project and the time she and her computer gave to the early stages of the graphics.

Ruth McCurry of Mowbray has been a challenging editor who has never failed me with her insight, constructive criticism and encouragement. In thanking her I also thank the many people who have read the typescript and suggested amendments, most of which have been incorporated in the text. They include those whose primary concern is evangelism, John Finney, the Church of England's Officer for the Decade of Evangelism, Anne Hibbert and Richard Zair of the Church Pastoral Aid Society; among the liturgists, Bishop Colin James, David Stancliffe, Colin Buchanan, Michael Perham, Kenneth Stevenson and Michael Vasey; and among those whose work is adult education, both clergy and lay formation, Clay Knowles, Richard Bainbridge and Kevin Eastell.

My thanks are also due for permission to quote from several authors in the course of the book. They are given credit in the text and details of their books are to be found in Chapter 9.

Throughout this book the general term 'minister' is used to refer to Anglican priests and deacons (usually known as rectors, vicars, curates or chaplains) and to priests, deacons and ministers of other denominations.

1

What Is the Adult Way to Faith?

This first chapter is written particularly for those who are leaders in their local church. It gives, I hope, enough of an outline of the 'Adult Way to Faith' for clergy and church council members to begin the work of deciding whether to adopt it. It ends with a worksheet offering suggestions to help a committee, a working party or project group to look more deeply at some of the issues that could be involved in their own community with the actual people who would be concerned.

What actually happens?

Instead of the clergy preparing adults for confirmation and baptism in the usual way, either individually or in a group, the Adult Way to Faith (catechumenate) has various special features:

The first feature is the involvement of lay people as group leaders and as sponsors of the new enquirers, together with the idea of a journey into faith in which lay people accompany new enquirers in their growth towards faith.

The second feature is the emphasis on the whole church community taking responsibility for such new enquirers, especially in welcoming them.

The third feature is that the Adult Way to Faith is divided into stages: stage 1 consists of preparatory sessions leading up to a celebration of welcome; stage 2 leads towards a first commitment and ends with a celebration of God's Call, in which those enquirers who are ready to go on towards baptism or confirmation are helped to understand that God is calling them; stage 3 involves further sessions leading up to baptism and confirmation (or a renewal of baptism promises for those who were baptized or confirmed in the past but recently have been following the Adult Way to Faith); stage 4, after confirmation, is a period of reflection and ministry, when people continue to meet and reflect on what has taken place and what God is calling them to do.

From the grassroots

One minister writes as follows:

> I regard my introduction to this movement as one of the most exciting
> events in over forty years of ministry. First meeting it at a conference for
> In-Service Training Officers, I was particularly impressed by the way some
> churches made preparation for baptism and confirmation a parish activity,
> with the congregation involved in the special services.
>
> I discussed the conference with a group of parishioners. There was a
> good deal of interest and I felt encouraged to take the matter further. We
> organized a residential parish weekend and discussed and prayed about the
> possibility of making the congregation responsible for preparation of
> adults. We decided to make a start with three candidates who were seeking
> confirmation. We selected sponsors. Candidates and sponsors made a
> public commitment during the Parish Communion, when our intentions
> were explained to the congregation. Ten members agreed to share in the
> programme. These and the sponsors made up two groups meeting once a
> fortnight.
>
> We decided to make a start in December and to admit candidates to Holy
> Communion the following Easter. This gave us Holy Week as a time of
> special preparation.
>
> Meetings were on Sunday evenings, lasted two hours, and were planned
> with the sponsors and helpers. We used an American manual as a basis,
> but adapted it freely.
>
> Before I left the parish we had three similar programmes with, to my joy,
> candidates from the first year becoming helpers in the following years. In
> the last year there were ten candidates and 45 helpers. In fact, a fair propor-
> tion of the congregation joined in. Since I left, the programme has con-
> tinued and is now in its eighth year.

A tool for evangelism

Both clergy and lay people are becoming more aware of the Church's
mission. We recognize that we have to be able to offer the Good News
to adult men and women. The Decade of Evangelism encourages us
to be open to new enquirers and to new ways of being the Church. In
this book I offer a way in which the Christian community in a parish
or some other institution can find a new and effective method of
accompanying enquirers into faith in Christ, to membership of the
Church, and to their part in the ministry of the people of God for the
coming of his rule on earth.

It is a method that has been working well in many different countries
for forty years. What I write is based on practical experience and the
evidence of people and parishes in a great variety of situations.

In the rest of the book I shall try to avoid using technical words, but
in order to put things in context I ought just to point out that the way
of working with people on their journey into faith described in this
book has various names. The title that I am going to use is 'the Adult
Way to Faith', or simply 'this Way' for short. However, you may find

other names used. Anglicans usually talk about 'the adult catechumenate' or simply 'the catechumenate'. In its Book of Occasional Services the Episcopal Church has a section on 'Preparing Adults for Holy Baptism' which offers guidance for the catechumenate and a series of short liturgies. The Roman Catholic Church has its Rite of Christian Initiation of Adults (usually referred to simply as RCIA).

This approach to coming to faith and joining the Christian Church has a very respectable history in the practice of the early Church in the first couple of centuries. The Church then was a minority movement in a largely pagan world, a situation that is shared today by most Christians in the various countries of the world.

Our Church in our age

Adult men and women at different stages of their lives ask searching questions about the meaning and purpose of life, and of their own lives in particular. There are many different groups offering answers to these questions in the market place as we near the end of the twentieth century. But it is still the case that enquirers come to the churches. In many churches the proportion of adults being confirmed continues to grow in comparison with the number of teenagers. This is true in spite of the fact that in most mainstream churches the figures for actual attendance at services are low.

The picture is mixed. On the one hand, the Church often looks out of place in the society in which it is set; it may seem tired, isolated, perhaps even lost. On the other hand, it does appear to have something to share that many men and women want. Our age is one in which the Churches have recognized that there is a need for explicit mission to the people of our own day and our own countries.

I hope this book will be of practical use to people of many churches. Its subject is adults and their search for faith in God and Christ. They approach the community of Christians for help and companionship on a journey that may end in full membership of the Body of Christ through the celebration of baptism or confirmation or some other sign of mature commitment to the faith and the Church of Jesus.

As an Anglican, I readily acknowledge that much of what I have to share in this book has come from modern Roman Catholic sources, but its roots lie deep in the shared Christian story of the early Church. And this process of growing in faith is a generally accepted part of all Christian bodies.

This Way is about conversion, faith in Christ, baptism and church membership. We recognize the activity of the Holy Spirit in a person, leading him or her towards God the Father through Jesus, to prayer and worship, and to a life lived in obedience to the love of God shown in his Son within a fellowship of people who share his mission in the world.

Some historical background

In the early centuries of the Christian Church, those who were in the first stages of their membership (known as 'catechumens' – people under instruction) were very carefully prepared for baptism. The Church then was a tiny minority movement, often subject to persecution by the state or other hostile factions. It was important that its members should be well prepared for the responsibilities, and the dangers, that being a member of the Christian community brought. Thus there was a time of preparation, often lasting several years, during which catechumens belonged to the family of the Church but not fully. They had joined but were not yet baptized, and they did not yet take part in the Eucharist.

This pattern of helping people into Christian life was in use for about two centuries in different forms in various places across the Mediterranean countries which made up the heart of the Roman Empire. In AD 313 the Emperor Constantine issued an edict legalizing Christianity, and within a short time it became the official religion of the Empire. This meant two things: first, there was no longer the same urgent need of courageous preparation for belonging to the Church, and secondly, there were lots more people wanting to join – especially when being baptized became a condition for jobs in the civil service or commissions in the army. So gradually the long and intense time of preparation fell out of use. The road to baptism became simpler, and baptism itself became more general.

We now leap forward to the twentieth century and to Roman Catholic missions in Africa. Here French missionary priests were looking for ways to train converts from other religions in the Christian way. They found their answer in their studies of the early Church. There, embedded like a fossil in Church history, was a tool waiting to be modernized and used. During and after the Second World War, leaders of the Church in France recognized that their nation was far from being a Christian country and launched the Mission to France. They too looked for ways to train the new Christians who were converted from among their own neighbours and found such ways in the experience of contemporary Africa and in that of the early Church.

The Second Vatican Council required that the catechumenate should be restored as part of the regular life of the Roman Catholic Church – not simply as a doctrinal preparation for baptism, but as 'a formation in the whole of Christian life and a sufficiently prolonged period of training'.

From the Anglican standpoint

Some Anglican clergy over the past fifty years have looked to the Catholic Church in France as the community where it has been easiest to have conversations across the denominational divide. In the 1940s there were many who acknowledged a debt to the inspiration of such books as Abbé Godin's *France Pagan?* and the efforts of the Mission de France in confronting the lack of interest in religion. This was a time when Christians in England had to come to terms with a similar situation in their own country. A Church of England report had been published in 1945 with a title in the same vein: *Towards the Conversion of England.* Anglicans also learned from the activities of the French catechumenate.

In the early 1970s there began a 'European Conference on the Catechumenate'. Centred largely on France and French-speaking countries, it has drawn together enthusiasts who were concerned to develop the method in their own countries. Almost from the start there has been an Anglican presence in this movement. The 1983 meeting was held in London under the joint auspices of Anglicans and Catholics. It was marked by a formal visit to the Archbishop of Canterbury at Lambeth Palace and a reception at Church House, Westminster, the centre of the General Synod of the Church of England.

Liturgies

The only official services for the initiation of adults in the Church of England are the baptism and confirmation liturgies in the Book of Common Prayer and the Alternative Service Book. The Episcopal Church of the USA gives its guidelines and outline liturgies in the Book of Occasional Services, mentioned above. The Church in South Africa also has a rite for the making of a catechumen.

Official statements

Some twenty years after the Second Vatican Council, the 1988 Anglican Lambeth Conference made an important recommendation in the section of its report dealing with mission and ministry under the heading 'Baptism'. Paragraph 199 reads:

> Preparation
>
> Just as we urge thorough preparation of parents for the baptism of an infant, so all the more we recommend thorough preparation of both candidates and sponsors at the baptism of an adult. Because it is entry into the missionary Body of Christ, baptism should lead, through the supportive fellowship of the Church, to a maturing process in the Spirit and to a sharing of Christ's ministry of service in the world. We note and commend a widespread interest in the revival of an adult Catechumenate and invite Provinces to consider the provision of guidelines for this.

In England the General Synod passed a motion at its February 1990 meeting:

> That this synod requests the House of Bishops, in the light of issues raised in the Knaresborough Report, *On Communion before Confirmation*, to consider

the case for reviving the catechumenate in order that adults, young people and infants may be associated with the Church, as a preliminary to Baptism, and for making provision for a draft order of service, whereby candidates would be admitted to such a catechumenate.

This was followed by the July 1991 General Synod resolution:

That this Synod . . . ask the House of Bishops in consultation with the Board of Education, Board of Mission and the Liturgical Commission to prepare a paper on patterns of nurture in faith, including the Catechumenate.

Also in 1991, the Anglican Liturgical Consultation, composed of representatives of provinces throughout the world, meeting in Toronto made the recommendation:

The Catechumenate is a model for preparation and formation for baptism. We recognize that its constituent liturgical rites may vary in different cultural circumstances.

Personal and parish experience

This brings me to my own story. I write this book because I am enthusiastic about the subject. I believe in the Adult Way to Faith for several reasons. They cluster around my experience that it works and two beliefs about its truth. First, I believe that it is true to the Gospel carried by the tradition of the Church to which I belong. Secondly, I believe that it is true also to the way men and women learn about the God of Jesus Christ and move, or are moved, to give their lives to his worship and service within the fellowship of his Church.

For nearly seventeen years I was rector of St Nicholas, Shepperton. This is a parish on the south-west of London, not far from Heathrow Airport. It is a largely residential area. The people who live there tend to work either in the centre of London or on its western edge, or in jobs connected with Heathrow. It was when I had been there for about three years that I met an Australian priest, Jim Cranswick, who in the course of work on a thesis about the catechumenate in the early Church had discovered that it was alive and flourishing in France. He had been given a commission to develop the approach and methods he had found there in a group of churches in the Kensington area of the London diocese. St Nicholas became one of these.

Over three years we gradually moved into a new way of preparing adults for confirmation. Until then, it had been the responsibility of the clergy, myself or the curate, to lead adult confirmation classes. The first change was to call in a small group of lay women and men who would act as guides to those preparing for confirmation. It was the start of a shared ministry in this area of the parish's work.

Initially I tended to ask people to work on a one-to-one basis, with an enquirer meeting with a church member over a period of several months. But a study leave which I spent visiting France, Switzerland

and Belgium to look at methods of training lay leaders persuaded me that this was too restrictive. Being the Church is about building and being a community. I realized that our method was short-changing the newcomers. They were not being introduced into an important dimension of discipleship: community. Thus we moved from a one-to-one basis to small groups.

Within a year or two a pattern developed. When there were, say, three or four people who wanted to enter more deeply into the faith, perhaps definitely thinking about being baptized or confirmed, I would ask a couple of people to lead a group for them. Sometimes this would be a husband and wife, but by no means always. We found it was a good thing to have two leaders, for they could help each other in preparing and reviewing the sessions, as well as providing variety in their approach. Along with the leaders and the enquirers there would be other people in the group. Sometimes members of the church would ask for a refresher course; sometimes I would have my eye on people as future group leaders. Such people would play an invaluable part in helping the new Christians on their journey, providing insight from their own experience as well as friendship and encouragement.

It was some time before we introduced any liturgical element. What first attracted me about the catechumenate was that it offered a very good pattern for adult Christian education. Later we began to experiment quite tentatively with little celebrations at the Parish Eucharist to welcome people at the beginning of their course and to pray with them as the time for their confirmation drew near.

I have since moved on to see that the formation side and the liturgical side of the process are dependent on each other; they work together for the candidate's growth towards Christian maturity within the community.

I left Shepperton to become a residentiary canon at St Paul's Cathedral. I have since resigned from that post to spend more time working with people from different churches, and I act as consultant to parishes as they begin to work along the lines outlined here. The approach of each parish varies, of course, with their different traditions and the different personalities involved; but I have been deeply impressed by the kind of testimony that all have given to the validity and genuineness both of the educational side of this Way and of the celebrations they have held with candidates and the congregation of their church.

Summary outline

So, what is this Way that I am so enthusiastic about? It is a way in which the Church accompanies men and women along the first stages of their journey into the Christian faith. For some this will lead to baptism, or the affirmation of their baptism in confirmation and holy communion, the sacrament that marks conversion and joining the

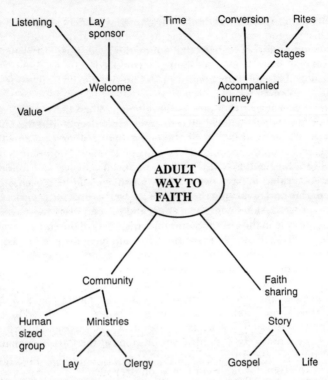

community. For others it may be a question of renewing a commitment to a belief and membership that was formally marked when they were much younger.

The first mark of this Way is *welcome*. It is an attitude that values the enquirer as the most important person in the process; that is marked by a real willingness to listen to her or him; and that respects the life stories which such enquirers bring, their interests, and the questions with which they come. The most obvious people to do this welcoming are the lay people of the church, and this ministry is expressed formally in the work of sponsors.

The second mark is an *accompanied journey into faith*. It has recognizable stages which can be celebrated in specially designed liturgies involving the congregation and the candidates.

Talk about a journey leads on to the third mark: this Way is concerned with *sharing faith* in God and Jesus Christ and uses that language rather than the language of Christian instruction. We are dealing with personal conversion rather than the acquisition of knowledge about religion. This takes a longer time than is usually envisaged with present-day confirmation courses.

Fourthly, experience has shown the great value of small groups as the place where new Christians can mature through experience of *the community* on a human scale. Community matters a great deal in this process. Candidates have come to join, or at least to test out, the community, the traditions it enshrines, and the message it has to share.

Members of the community can have many different ministries within the process. In particular, there is a variety of lay ministries which may seem to take over from the clergy much of what, in the past, they have considered their province. Lay leaders are responsible for accompanying and directing the enquirers in their groups.

The clergy can discover a new role as leaders of lay teams, exercising their calling as pastors and teachers in a fresh way through encouraging, training and enabling the members of the community to 'be the Church' in their own place.

Sponsors take on the role of friends and pastors to new Christians. The whole congregation is invited (or challenged) to accept responsibility for welcome, for support, and for the encouragement of their prayers.

Why change?

Over the years I have found that different sorts of people respond to different arguments for changing to this Way. There is often, quite simply, a sense of dissatisfaction with what is happening at present, an awareness that adults are not getting all that they should from their confirmation classes. There are some who are encouraged by the evidence from other parishes and communities that this method works: that people who have gone through the process develop into mature Christians; that the quality of church life in the parish seems to deepen. There are others who are impressed by the Roman Catholic rite and by the way it has taken root in parishes.

In the final resort, though, it is only through personal experience and the experience of your own church that you can really measure the worth of what is on offer here. It is a case of 'suck it and see'. That is why the worksheets are a built-in part of this book. If you do begin to adopt this Way, then please remember that you need to be part of the process of change. As James Dunning, one of the leading lights in the movement, says: 'The great commandment here is "Thou shalt not do unto others what thou hast not done for thyself"'.

Parish stories

A suburban minister writes:

> We had our confirmation on the night of Easter Eve with some sixteen adults being confirmed and some of them baptized. We had two groups, one led by lay people and one led by me and a lay person. They began in September and went on officially till the following September, but they still continue unofficially as groups of friends meeting about once a month. It has been a wonderful year for leaders, candidates and sponsors; everyone has got such a lot from the experience.

Another group has now been formed under the leadership of two different lay people and we are planning for a confirmation on Whitsunday
morning. The group is very mixed and we haven't yet moved to the point
where they are to be introduced to the congregation and matched up with
sponsors; some of them are sitting very delicately on the edge of the church
and I am having to play it very carefully by ear.

This is just to say that we are continuing here at St Mary's and it is gently
and gradually transforming the parish.

A lay leader from another parish writes:

The two cycles here had very different participants. The first year had a
group of men and women in their sixties and seventies, the second a group
in their middle to late twenties. We met for two and a half hours each
Wednesday. After initial awkwardness and hesitancy for about two weeks,
the commitment of both groups warmed the feeling of community. The
spirit was very much one of a voyage, an adventure, a journey, a pilgrimage into the unknown.

The unpredictable prospects of the weeks yet to come tended to draw us
closer to each other. The younger group grew in maturity and conversely
the older group grew more excitable and young again, as if years were fall-
ing off them and they could start life again. Humour and honesty flowed
out. It was revealing to watch someone of sixty coming to learn about God
for the first time suddenly realize that God had intervened in their life
unbeknown to them perhaps some thirty years earlier. The younger people
were more interested in 'technical' questions, picking passages of scripture
apart to get the meanings out.

I admit to a feeling of great pleasure and satisfaction myself in being able
to take part. They taught me just as much as I taught them. It was a great
moment to go with them to the cathedral on their confirmation day.

Worksheet

Having read thus far, you may find it helpful to look at Worksheet 1.
It is designed for those who have responsibility in the parish, and may
raise questions to bear in mind as you read the next two chapters.

Worksheet 1:
How to Start

For the church council or committee who are deciding what to do about adults coming into the church.

Preliminary work

Read Chapter 1.

Task

The group should meet, perhaps more than once, with the following tasks:

1. Work through these questions and any others that come out of the discussions:

(a) What is the current position in your church concerning adult enquirers? How does the church meet them? What is the quality of welcome? How many adults are confirmed? How are they prepared? What are your feelings and comments about what happens at present?

(b) Having read about the Adult Way to Faith, what does it offer to your church? How well would it suit your church?

(c) If you believe your church should adopt this method, what are the decisions that have to be made?

(d) Who should take those decisions?

(e) What do you think are the main differences between what happens now and what the Adult Way to Faith offers? What changes would need to be made?

(f) What problems have you already encountered and what problems do you anticipate?

(g) How could you meet these problems?

2. Come to a formal decision as to whether to adopt or to recommend to the appropriate body that your church adopts the Adult Way to Faith.

3. If you decide in favour, arrange dates for two planning meetings.

2

A Welcoming Church

Who is this for?

This chapter is written particularly for the people who have to make decisions in the life of the local church: for those involved in planning and putting into action the changes that the Adult Way to Faith may mean in your particular place. The chapter contains a series of worksheets to help you earth the subject in your own situation and see what action needs to be taken.

The background

We live in a world that has seen nearly two thousand years of Christianity. For much of that time the culture of many countries has been avowedly Christian. Systems of government have proclaimed themselves Christian; indeed, some have been dominated by the Church. In the United Kingdom there are established Churches. The teaching of religion, and in particular the teaching of Christianity, has a special place in the state education system. There is certainly a widespread layer of what is often called 'folk religion'.

A 1988 report commissioned by the Independent Broadcasting Authority, *Godwatching*, points to this when it says: 'Claimed membership of any Christian faith accounted for 79 per cent of people. Even amongst people who are not at all religious, two out of three described themselves as "Christians".'

However, a rather harsher picture of the practice of Christianity in Britain comes from the MARC survey *Christian Britain?* Quoting George Gallup, it says 'The gulf between what we believe in our heads and what we feel in our hearts and practise in our lives is growing wider'. The English Church Census records the returns from a large number of places of Christian worship of the numbers of churchgoers on 14 October 1989. It gives comparisons with several similar surveys over the preceding 14 years. They show that the percentage of churchgoers in the adult population in 1989 was 9.5 per cent, a decline from 11.3 per cent in 1975. This suggests that in each year over that period, something like 28,000 people stopped going to church. 'The figures represent two people per thousand in the population who no longer attend. That is hardly a rapid decline: the church is not going to roll over and die.'

If you are interested enough to read as far as this, it is probably because you recognize that even if this experience of overall decline in numbers is true in your own church, there are still newcomers who want to join. So who are they?

Those men and women who discover a living and active faith as adults may have had several sorts of contact with Christianity and the Church along the way. It is different from the days of the early Church; we are not often faced with people for whom the teachings of Jesus or the fact of the Church are totally new. There will often be some kind of prehistory of faith or knowledge.

It is also unlikely that those who come to enquire at the local church will be at the beginning of the journey of sacramental initiation into the Church. Christening babies may not be as regular a practice as it was: the statistics for all churches show a dramatic decline over the last 20 years in the number of infants baptized compared with the number of babies born. But the experience of most parishes is that we more often deal with adult preparation for confirmation rather than for baptism. A few of the candidates may not have been baptized as babies, but they are comparatively rare.

This variety of people's experience and the wide range of their religious positions point to the need we shall encounter over and over again: the need to be adaptable in responding to people's circumstances, to new events, and changing situations.

Our main concern here is with people in the early stages of adult faith. I hear regularly from leaders and helpers as well as from parish clergy about the wonderful effects that taking part in the programme has had on church life and on the individual discipleship of church members. But this is not the purpose of the scheme. The Adult Way to Faith is not a programme for parish renewal or for deepening the faith of church members, however much it may also have those valuable results. It exists first and foremost for enquirers, for newcomers to the Church, for candidates.

Why do people come?

As I look round congregations I have served I recognize that the events of family life often lead people towards the Church. When a baby is born, the parents want a christening. The feelings of joy and gratitude at the birth of a baby, coupled with the recognition of responsibility, often evoke some sort of religious response.

Children at primary school ask questions, want to join Sunday School perhaps. Parents may feel they need more in the way of knowledge if they are to answer or support their son or daughter. Parishes that have a church school know the pressure there can be on places. Parents who originally come to church for ulterior motives may find that they stay out of conviction!

Preparing for a wedding may move a young couple to think more deeply about faith as they look forward to the prospect of their life together. For many it is their first experience of meeting the Church.

Illness, death and bereavement are part of the other side of life that brings people into contact with the Church. Most families expect a religious funeral service in church or at the local crematorium. There may also be counselling available to help a person through grief.

There are other hurts, too. It may be the pain of marriage break-up or problems between parents and children; unemployment and debt; perhaps the weight of alcoholism or drug addiction; not to mention the many named or nameless fears, anxieties and depressions that darken so many lives.

Because of the speed and frequency with which people move round the country, many are lonely. They need to find a way to make friends. The local church can often provide an opportunity for meeting others through services or through clubs and organizations.

At some point in their journey through life, most human beings ask what it all means, what is the point of it all? This search for meaning and purpose in life brings many into contact with the Church.

Alongside these and the many other events in life that draw or push people towards the Church, there are people whose need is religious or spiritual. They sense a desire for God, and they want to know more about Jesus.

The Christian offer

The next thing is to ask how your church responds to these men and women who come with their expectations and demands, how it welcomes the gifts that they bring.

There's a saying, 'You don't get a second chance to make a first impression'. It should be written in big bold letters on the walls of clergy vestries and at the head of the quarterly rotas of churchwardens, sidesmen and sideswomen, Sunday greeters and welcoming teams!

Try to put yourself in the shoes of a new enquirer coming to your church and sense what he or she may experience. How would it strike you? (Perhaps, how *did* it strike you when you were new?) Would you use words like 'friendly'? 'warm'? 'embarrassing'? 'scary'? 'unwelcoming'?

We are talking here about first contacts, about wedding bookings or passport application signatures, arrangements for a funeral after a tragic, pointless road accident, or an enquiry about which day the Mothers' and Toddlers' group meets. The point is to look at the

quality of welcome that marks out the life of your church and the
people who are its public face.

God loves

The infinite value of each child of God should be the mark of the way
Christians treat the people they meet. This is easily said, but very
much harder to put into practice.

People matter, and so does everything about them. We all have our
own story, our own background. Our social class is part of how we
approach the world around us. We are at home with the things we
are at home with: jobs and leisure activities; favourite television
programmes and Sunday papers; sports or hobbies. We are at home
with the kind of people we get on with, too. And we are used to the
way in which we try to make sense of life in general – what in the
broadest sense can be called our faith.

Looking first at the negative side, it is worth asking whether the
church to which you belong devalues any of those aspects of a person's
life and surroundings. Who is unwelcome? It is a hard question to ask
of a Christian community, but it has to be faced. There are limits to
what a group can tolerate. Scandal, fears, snobbery, shyness, embarrassment and dislikes are things that are common to most people –
Christians included. Where do you and your friends at church draw
back from meeting people who upset or threaten you?

Look on the positive side, however, and see what welcome can
mean. The God I meet in Jesus Christ is a God who loves people. He
loves them as they are here and now. He also sees the full potential
that they are capable of growing into with his help. He is a God who
forgives and heals. We call Jesus 'Our Saviour'. New Testament
writers occasionally used the same word for 'saving' and for 'healing'.
In the stories of Jesus meeting, healing and saving people there is a
constantly recurring theme of his acceptance and love meeting people
whose experience of life was one of rejection and dismissal. Is your
church one of those churches where people come for help and for healing of one sort or another? Do people find there what they are looking
for? If they do, can you say how it happens?

Listen!

You may use the words 'evangelism' or 'evangelization' to describe
the work of the Church and of individual Christians presenting the
Gospel to people and accompanying them along the way that leads into
Christian faith. Whichever word you use, I believe this work has to
begin with welcome. The first step in evangelism must be respect for
the other person. True evangelists are people with big ears and big
hearts. They are not necessarily people with big mouths!

Welcome is vital for two reasons. Without it, newcomers are put off.

They feel unwanted, they sense a lack of respect, and they have to be very brave or very determined to keep on coming back for what they need. They can just as easily go away. Welcome is also vital for the basic Christian reason that it reflects the way God deals with us. The Gospel is about God going out of his way to be with us, to give each human being the respect that is part of his love for her or for him.

A church that is effective in mission, which has taken to heart the call to evangelize, and within which people are able to learn, is a church whose members have learnt how to listen. This does not always come easily. It is a skill that most of us have to take the trouble to prac-tise. It requires attitudes that run counter to much of the culture around us.

Listening demands a real respect for the other person and for their ideas, their character and their habits. It requires unselfishness in a culture that celebrates individual achievement and success above caring and generosity.

Listening is also a skill that can be improved through exercises. There should be opportunities for this near you. It is worth making the effort to develop your understanding of how you come across as a speaker and as a listener, how much 'body language' matters, and how you feel when you yourself are not being listened to properly.

The welcoming church

The obvious public occasion for judging the quality of your church's welcome is when someone new comes to a service. The questions concern the friendliness of the people who do the greeting at the door, the atmosphere of the congregation at worship, and what could be called the 'accessibility' of the whole occasion – how easy or difficult it is to enter into what goes on.

The same questions could be asked about a church social evening, badminton club, or youth fellowship.

Telephones are a vitally important means of welcome in the modern world. How is the phone answered at your vicarage, presbytery, manse or parish office?

Alongside this official face of your church, there is another far more important (but less obvious) area for welcome. It is in the everyday contacts between church men and women and the people they meet as they go about their daily lives. These are the real missionaries and it is their attitudes that matter as much as the official ones. Church people and their homes can be the key to effective welcome.

'Open spaces' round the church

This consideration of the quality of welcome leads on to thinking about the way a church organizes itself for welcome. Look at your own church and think about other churches you know; you may well recognize this sort of pattern:

1. There is a core of committed church people; they are regular attenders; they provide money through stewardship or planned giving; they take responsibility for the leadership of different aspects of church life and for the management of its affairs.

2. The less committed people are a larger group. There is no doubt that they belong. They are church attenders who take part in activities connected with the church, but they are not at the heart of things.

3. There is a large number of occasional attenders. They would be extremely hurt to be told that they did not belong to their local church, because they think of themselves as members, even if the keener church people might question the depth of their commitment.

4. Then there is the fringe. A great many people have connections with the church. Perhaps it is a childhood connection through Sunday School. I am forever amazed by the number of people, men in particular, who seem to think that they will get into heaven, or at least count as members of the Church, on the strength of having played football with a great curate in the Youth Club!

5. For many people it is something to do with family; their children are in the church school or are Cub Scouts and Brownies in the church Pack. Churches often have clubs, day centres or playgroups in their halls and people come into contact with the church through these.

Thus there is a kind of 'open space' around the church, an uncommitted place where contacts with a low level of commitment can occur between men and women and the Christian community. It is here that most evangelism actually takes place, whether formally or in a quite informal way. It is a place of enquiry.

Time of enquiry

This 'open space' round the church, where people meet Christians and test out for themselves whether the community and the things it stands for are likely to be attractive, provides the opportunity for evangelization. It is not for most people a formal stage in their approach to the church. There are no set ways by which people come, though there may be similarities. So there are no set ways for parishes to meet them. There is a very wide variety of ways in which different church communities manage this stage of enquiry. Some parishes hold organized meetings for newcomers to get together with the church and to find out answers to their initial questions. Others begin very early to establish the preparation groups with sponsors and enquirers. Others, again, rely on the informal contacts between people and church members or the clergy.

Whatever method is adopted, this is a time for telling about our lives and learning about the lives of others. It is a time when the church can hear the questions asked by enquirers. It is a time for simply getting to know people, learning where they come from, what their life is like, and where their interests lie. It is also a time for the first presentations of the message of the Church.

This 'getting to know' is a two-way process. People have come to find out about Christianity and the Christian community in the local church. They want to test it out for themselves to see whether it offers an answer to their questions or a way of meeting their own particular needs. Sometimes they may need a good deal of help in recognizing and putting these needs into words. Many people have to be helped towards acknowledging their need for reconciliation with God.

The church person is in a position to share the Gospel with them. But sensitively. The leader of a group of enquirers is advised to keep a notebook in which to write down after each meeting just what the people were asking or saying about faith, putting it in the actual words they used. This is so that when it comes to responding with answers from the Gospel, she or he can use words and phrases that have come from the others and are part of their vocabulary. Listening matters as the first act in communication. In the communication of the Gospel that is evangelization, it is vitally important.

The lay person's ministry

The rest of this book is about how ordinary, regular worshippers can become better able to share the Christian faith with those who approach the Church to discover what it stands for; to find answers to their questions; or to have their particular need met by the community which stands for the God who showed his love in the life, death and resurrection of Jesus Christ and who continues to show that love today.

The most important tool that the Church has in this work of evangelism is the people who make up its membership. That is why it matters so much that their strengths, their insights and their experience should be valued and developed. What is more, they have both the responsibility and the authority for exercising this ministry in their own baptism.

I keep coming back to sentences in the introduction to the Roman Catholic Rite of Christian Initiation of Adults (para. XXI):

> The people of God, as represented by the local Church, should understand and show by their concern that the initiation of adults is the responsibility of all the baptized. Therefore the community must always be fully prepared in the pursuit of its apostolic vocation to give help to those who are searching for Christ. In the various circumstances of daily life, even as in the apostolate, all the followers of Christ have the obligation of spreading the faith according to their abilities.

Gospel

The dialogue of evangelism may begin - very often *does* begin, and perhaps always *should* begin - with the Church listening to the enquirer. But it is a dialogue. The Church has its news to tell. The Christian has something to offer to meet the need, respond to the question, or awaken the awareness of the other person. You may notice that I swing between using 'Church' and 'Christian' between the organization and the individual. This is intentional. Both personal experience and collective experience are involved. There is the story that the Christian community has to tell. This tradition is carried in the Old and New Testaments with the stories of God's communities and the events that happened to them - and, above all, the story of Jesus. It continues in the churches to which we belong in these last few years of the twentieth century. As members of the community of faith, we have something bigger than ourselves to hand on to new people.

But we also have our own personal and individual story to tell and our own personal and individual faith to share. If you have read as far as this, I can assume you have some interest in the subject. You may not believe that your interest is worth a great deal. If I asked you to speak about your faith, you might well say that it was very weak and you'd rather not say anything. I respect your reticence, but I suggest you make the jump!

In St Luke's gospel you will find the account of the two disciples walking to Emmaus on the first Easter evening and their meeting with the risen Jesus. It gives a remarkable example of this mixture of personal experience and the deep roots of tradition. There is both the disciples' eye-opening awareness that it is Jesus alive and with them, and their recognition of the immediacy and relevance of the Scriptures that he opens to them. Their response is to rush back to the others and shout about their new faith.

Worksheet 2A:
Are We a Welcoming Church?

For the same group as Worksheet 1.

Preliminary work

Read the section 'Why do people come?' on pages 13–14.

Task

1. Consider the people who have joined the church in the last year.
    (a) Who were they?
    (b) What have they said about their reasons for coming?
    (c) What attracted them?
    (d) What kind of background do they come from?
    (e) Did they have church contacts before?
2. How did *we* come into the Church? Tell each other in pairs or small groups and record your findings.
3. Answer the following questions:
    (a) How do people in your area get to know about your church?
    (b) What information is made available and how?
    (c) Where would local people go if they wanted information?
    (d) How would they know where to go?
    (e) What are the points of contact for adults? For children?

Worksheet 2B:
How We Welcome

Preparatory work

Read the section 'The Christian offer' on pages 14–15.

Task

1. As a whole group, or in twos, threes or fours, answer these questions:

(a) What kind of experience might someone have who telephoned the vicarage, presbytery or church office?

(b) What kind of experience might they have if they knocked on the door of the vicarage, presbytery or church office?

(c) . . . if they came along to a service?

(d) . . . if they came to a meeting of a church organization?

2. List anything that might make people feel unwelcome.

(a) Are there people you would be surprised to see in church?

(b) Any particular age group?

(c) Any particular type of person?

3. Are there ways in which your parish could do better at:

(a) Publicity and informing people?

(b) Getting into contact with people?

(c) Welcoming newcomers?

(d) Helping them to feel at home?

(e) Accepting the unlikely people?

(f) Listening to what people really have to say?

Worksheet 2C:
The Shape of Your Church

Preparation

Read the section ' "Open spaces" round the church' on pages 16–17.

Task

Work through these questions together:

1. Do you recognize this description of a church? Is yours similar or different?

2. Do you have a core of committed church people?

3. Do you have people who attend church but are not at the centre of things?

4. Do you have people who come occasionally?

5. Do you have people who have links with the church but don't come to services?

6. What kinds of links are you aware of?

Worksheet 2D:
Listening

Preparation

Read the section 'Time of enquiry' on pages 17-18.

Task

Either

1. Working in pairs, try this imaginative exercise:

   One member of the pair is a church member. The other has come to church for the first time but wants to talk about what is on his or her mind. (It may be a bereavement, a financial or family problem, concern to bring up a child properly, the baptism of a baby, or something joyful they want to share.)

   Role play the conversation between the two. Then review the conversation.

   (a) Did the 'newcomer' feel the 'church person' was welcoming? A good listener?

   (b) What can the 'church person' remember and re-tell about the 'newcomer's' concerns?

Or

2. Another exercise in pairs:

   Being yourselves and not pretending or imagining anything, tell each other how you reached your personal faith.

   Who inspired you?

   taught you?

   welcomed you? etc.

Then review the conversation.

   (a) How were you listened to?

   (b) What did it feel like to be the listener? Easy or hard?

   (c) What did it feel like to be telling your story?

3

Companions along the Way

This chapter is about the ministry that sponsors and other lay people engaged in the Adult Way to Faith are asked to undertake. It is about the central idea of a journey into the Christian faith which for some people leads to church membership. It closes with two worksheets. Worksheet 3A is for the group that has the responsibility for introducing the Adult Way to Faith in the parish. Worksheet 3B gives outlines for one session (or, preferably, two) of the preparation and training of people who are to be sponsors and group leaders.

Many people following the Adult Way to Faith will be preparing for confirmation. For others, the goal will be baptism. For some who were baptized and confirmed earlier in life it will be a way leading to a celebration that reaffirms their adult faith. Each will be on a journey that is private and individual to them. But just as different people have a similar sort of skeleton, so there are likely to be similar elements in different people's journeys. The details vary, but there are elements common to all.

The journey starts at a time when people have little personal belief in God and Jesus, or perhaps none at all. It leads to a point where they can make a personal commitment of trust and belief and become active members of the Church. The journey also, of course, carries the possibility that people may decide not to continue and to opt out.

Journey language

Speaking about a journey marks something of a change from much established church practice. In my church it is usual to talk of 'confirmation classes', where the very name tends to convey a picture of school and education. For most ordinary people this means being told about things. There are teachers and there are pupils: people who know and people who are ignorant and need to be taught. For many adults these images and phrases immediately call up a sense of failure and inadequacy. It is sad but true that grown men and women can feel threatened by the idea of learning.

When we talk about an accompanied journey, we are offering a different image from that of school with its difficult echoes. We are talking about travelling along a road with a companion who is there not as a teacher but as a guide. It is walking with a friend who has herself or himself already travelled their own road and knows some of the features of yours.

Journey also implies movement and change. Certainly there is knowledge to be shared and there will be questions to face, but the real work is in the many-sided personal changes that are conversion to Christ. You start from where you are and move on through each successive point on the road to the place you are going to.

It sounds simple, but each part of that last sentence is very important. You can only begin where you are. For the accompanying person, this is a matter of listening sufficiently carefully to discern what their friend's present position is, what they believe, what they find difficult. They need to listen in order to understand the questions and what lies behind them.

Where people are is their present gift from God. Church people can easily fall into the danger of being so full of the truth which they believe God has given them that they simply have to tell it first, before listening to the other person. It is no bad thing to remember that God has been there already; *is* there already. We do not bring God to the new Christian. One of our jobs is to help the enquirers to see where he is at work in their lives and in their hearts.

The idea of journey extends far wider than simply learning with your mind about Christianity and the Church. It is about entering into a relationship with God that changes the way you live. It has a bearing upon your understanding, your feelings, your experience of life, your attitudes and the choices you make.

The shift is from thinking in terms of instruction to thinking about conversion. It is about how people make changes, how they respond to new experiences and relationships, as they enter into new awareness of the Christian faith and the Christian community. It is about growth towards maturity as a disciple of Jesus.

How long?

Time is another area where you may find differences from what has been the accepted practice of your church. A course of preparation for confirmation might be expected to run for about two or three months. During that time people would have sessions on the main teachings of the Church. It is possible that they may follow a course laid down in a handbook. The assumption is that they will be ready for confirmation when they have finished the course. They will be reckoned to know enough.

In the Adult Way to Faith, 'knowing enough' is certainly important, but the signs of conversion are vital. What matters is a deepening
relationship with and commitment to Jesus Christ. This will show
itself in an altered pattern of life as someone comes to accept that the
way they believe affects their everyday behaviour. Once you accept
that, you move into a different time scale. The pattern of acquiring
knowledge through attendance at classes switches to one of personal
change. This is a far slower process. It deals with attitudes, relationships and things of the spirit. The rhythm is far more leisurely than
that of head-knowledge. Instead of a couple of months, we can be looking at a journey that may take a year or more.

To change the pattern of confirmation preparation like this may
seem something of a threat. Candidates may feel impatient, especially
when their friends went through the process much faster last year. The
clergy may feel they are asking too much. But it is true that the best
witnesses for this extended time are the candidates themselves. People
who have been given the space to grow and mature through the Way
tend to feel very sorry for the others who rushed the job under the old
system.

Commonly, groups will meet for most of the church's working
season, which starts when the schools go back after the summer
holidays and leads up to Easter. This would be particularly the case
in the churches where the Easter Vigil is the time for baptism and confirmation. For some people it may be right to think of a period that
is a great deal longer. For others it may be shorter. Programmes,
calendars and timetables are convenient tools in all this, but they
should never be allowed to become straitjackets.

'Accompanied'

When most Christians tell the story of how they came to the Christian
faith or joined their church, they talk about friends, the men and
women through whom they began to discover God in Jesus, and the
fellowship of the community of believers. Only a minority will talk
about doctrines and statements about belief. The way Christian faith
is described and handed on in words is important, but for the vast
majority of enquirers and new believers what matters most is other
people. Ask them what it was that attracted them and held their
interest and you will hear about welcome, acceptance, friendship,
warmth, inspiration and example.

We recognize these different kinds of experience and build on them.
People approaching the faith or the church need companionship. This
is best given by lay members of the church. 'Sponsor' is the word used
to describe the more experienced Christian friend who accompanies
an enquirer.

Sponsors stand as representatives of the church. So it is usual for
them to be invited by the parish clergy. It may happen that a candidate

has in mind someone they would particularly like to choose as their sponsor, but it is always important that their choice is endorsed by the church. On the whole, it is probably best not to have a member of the enquirer's own family as a sponsor.

There are several different ways in which parishes use sponsors. Some have a one-to-one link between a candidate and his or her sponsor. Sponsors take a full part in the group meetings with their candidate as well as spending time with them privately.

In others, sponsors may not be members of the group that meets regularly to work with the candidates, but will have an important role to play in talking through afterwards what has come up in the meetings.

There are also parishes that do not work with one-to-one sponsoring, but rather see the group as the context in which the support and befriending take place. In this case, a group would be made up of candidates and church people together.

We shall be dealing more fully with how these groups might work in the next two chapters. For the present I simply want to note how important they are for someone who is making their way along the faith journey. The meetings, the way people enter into conversation about things that matter deeply to them, and the friendships that grow over the weeks and months are a vital element.

Conversion

Conversion is about changing direction. A convert is a person who has turned or been turned. This makes it a very good family of words to use when we talk about a journey into faith. Along that journey there are plenty of moments when decisions have to be made. There is the first decision to start on the journey at all, a conscious choice to turn away from a life without God in order to seek him and his meaning for oneself. It is a process of personal change. There are many ways of describing it: growing in Christ-likeness, being conformed to the image of Christ, or developing into the person that God has designed you to become.

In this change Christians have always recognized that there is a dialogue going on. Conversion is something that God effects in a person's life. It is God's initiative. On the other hand, the human person is not simply a passive object. We have been given a power of choice. Conversion is something in which each man and woman is involved. We can respond with a 'Yes' or a 'No' to God's initiative. In conversion, God turns us, changes our direction. But we also have a responsibility of our own to choose to turn in that new direction.

There is a variety of kinds of conversion in the New Testament. It's not all Paul-on-the-road-to-Damascus, by any means. His sudden blinding awareness of Jesus Christ and of his own need to respond to him have been repeated in the lives of people throughout the ages, but that is by no means the only pattern of conversion. Consider, for example, the calling of Andrew, Peter, James and John from their work as fishermen, or the friendship of Mary and Martha with Jesus. Each of them grew in making a faithful response to Jesus, but in different ways. These ways give us different pictures of conversion.

Step by step and stage by stage

Everyone's journey into Christian faith is different. It is personal and affected by all sorts of individual characteristics and outward circumstances. But most people can recognize that they have aspects in common with one another. The Adult Way to Faith recognizes these common points and celebrates them in the liturgical rites which it offers at different moments.

The Way really begins when someone moves from the stage of checking out the Church, from sniffing round what it has to offer, to some kind of request for deepening faith, more understanding or closer membership.

Stories

I am thinking of people like Fred, who nursed his wife for seven months at home before she died. His first real contact with the church came over her funeral, when he found that the care he received was a great help. He had made friends at the British Legion Club since he retired, but there was something about the service in church and the friendship that he began to experience from the minister and one of the men in the church which seemed to touch him at a deeper level than he found in the Club. Somehow he felt he wanted to get a little closer to whatever it was that seemed to help in his grief.

Kathy had never been christened, so when she came with Tim to arrange to get married at St Stephen's she was really very nervous. She didn't know if she could have a church wedding if she wasn't baptized. When the curate said she could still be baptized, even though she was an adult, she agreed that it would be a good idea, and decided to join the classes. Tim did, too.

Bernard was a successful businessman. Over the years he had made a good deal of money. He and his wife had a nice house in the suburbs and a holiday home in the country. The children had completed their education and were living away from home. But what was it all for? Nice to be a two-car, two-home husband and wife, but what really was the point of life?

Cynthia had been away for a short holiday in Yorkshire. Early one morning she and her friend visited York Minster. It was quiet with not many people about, just somebody softly playing the organ. She felt something happen to her that she couldn't really explain. She knew

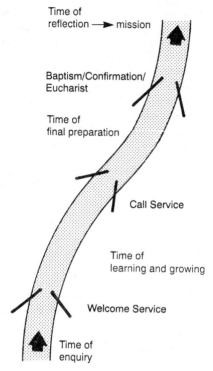

Time of
reflection ➤ mission

Baptism/Confirmation/
Eucharist

Time of
final preparation

Call Service

Time of
learning and growing

Welcome Service

Time of
enquiry

A MAP OF THE JOURNEY

it was true and lovely and real. It felt very good. It was like wanting something very much and getting it at the same time, but not being able to explain it. If this was God, she wanted more.

There are as many stories as there are people. There is a point where a person, faced with something like one of these experiences, makes a move towards the Church. They might speak with a Christian friend or turn up at church. They might even pick up the phone to make an appointment to see the minister. In one way or another, they make a definite first enquiring step on the journey.

The journey that different people travel in the Christian faith, the journey of conversion, has recognizably different phases and periods of developing growth and discovery. In the Adult Way to Faith, changes from one period or phase to another can be marked by special services or rites celebrated in church.

Service of welcome

The Way starts when a group of enquirers and sponsors or helpers is formed and the members begin their journey together. This beginning

can be celebrated in church. I remember one young woman saying to
me after a few weeks of group meetings 'Is there anything to show
we've started?' In a liturgy such as this she could experience just that.

The Service of Welcome celebrates a desire to find out about the
Christian faith. The commitment is to a search; it is not yet a commitment to formal membership or to baptism or confirmation. That may
be the final outcome, but for most people it is more a matter of 'I want
to go a bit further before I decide. I need to know some more, be more
convinced that it's right for me.' The church too is aware that the
enquirers are just taking early steps along a way that may lead them
to full membership of the Christian community.

You will see suggested outlines for the rite in Chapter 8. It is
designed to do several things:

1. The enquirers are taking an important first step at the beginning
of faith and commitment. They are turning towards God and the
life of a Christian. They are asking something of the Christian community, their local church. This service gives formal expression to
where they are in their journey of faith.

2. In this service the local church welcomes the new people and
accepts their commitment to explore faith and membership. Their
sponsors need to be seen to have a ministry within the church, so this
could be the occasion for them to be commissioned.

3. The rite is not centred only on people and the local community.
It is also a time for prayer and for God's blessing expressed in giving
the enquirers the sign of the cross.

4. The local church meets to recognize the new enquirers; it joins
in prayer with and for them. The witness of the new people who want
to join their community can often challenge regular churchgoers to
look again at the way they live out their own beliefs.

Learning and growing time

There comes a time in the faith journey when people recognize that
they can no longer sit on the edge. They have either to walk away or
to jump in. The time of enquiry in the 'open spaces' surrounding the
church leads in due course to a moment of choice and decision. For
some people it is a movement of the Spirit within themselves. They
'know' they must do something about it. For others, the pressure
comes from other people or from outside events.

The Service of Welcome celebrates a first commitment to the
Church and to a journey of learning and growing in the faith of Jesus
Christ. It is like being engaged. It is not yet a full membership, but
it is a belonging rather than a standing outside looking in.

It leads into the period during which the enquirers and the people
who are accompanying them get down to hearing the story of the
Christian Gospel and relating that to the realities of their own lives and

their own situations. We shall look more closely at this sharing of faith
in Chapters 4 and 5.

Different people will take different amounts of time over this.
Ideally the length of a course and what it contains should be tailored
to fit every individual, because the enquirer is the central person in
all that the Adult Way to Faith stands for. However, life rarely allows
for that and adjustments have to be made so that as many as possible
can travel together.

God who calls

The tradition that Easter is the time for baptism goes right back to the
early Church. St Paul, writing in Romans 6, clearly links baptism to
Jesus' death and resurrection. There is a dying to an old way of life
without faith, and a being born, or rising from death, into a new life
in Christ. In the Church's year there are other special days that are
also particularly suitable for baptizing people. The season of Epiphany
celebrates the baptism of Jesus; Whitsun recalls the gift of the Holy
Spirit to the Church and the baptism of those who responded to the
preaching of Peter; All Saints is the time for remembering fellowship
with all the faithful who over the centuries have been baptized into
Christ.

Before a man or woman is baptized or confirmed, choices have to
be made. Both the candidate and the local church need to be sure that
this is the right step for them to be taking at this particular time. It
may not be. He or she may not be ready to make such a commitment.

There are several people involved in discerning their readiness.
There are the candidates themselves, those who accompany them, and
the parish clergy. In the early Church it would have been the bishop
who made the final decision whether or not to admit this person to the
Church through baptism, and the bishop still has an important role
to play today in the process of initiation.

This acceptance of the readiness of people for initiation can be
celebrated in a service that is centred on the theme of God's Call. The
focus of the liturgy is on the God who called Abraham, and who called
Moses, the God who chose the holy nation. It looks to Jesus who called
his disciples and invited them to be with him before he sent them out
to be his messengers. It proclaims the same God who through baptism
and the Eucharist calls men and women today to be 'a chosen race,
a royal priesthood, a dedicated nation, a people claimed by God for
his own, to proclaim the glorious deeds of him who has called you out
of darkness into his marvellous light'. Chapter 8 gives examples of the
service of God's Call. The people who have spent time growing in the
Christian faith, in their understanding of what it means to belong to
the Church and in their awareness of the demands of their new faith
upon their ordinary life and service of others, are now commended by

their sponsors and other people in the Church to be baptized or confirmed at the celebration in a few weeks' time.

Period of spiritual preparation

The season of Lent was originally the time when candidates made their final spiritual preparation in prayer and fasting before their baptism as Easter. Whether or not the baptism or the confirmation in your church takes place at Easter, there should be some kind of special preparation for the candidates. The early Christians called it a time of 'enlightenment'. Just as Jesus withdrew from the busyness of his ministry to pray in the mountains before times of important decisions or special work, so this can be a time for particular emphasis on prayer. Themes may well include recognizing the challenges that the coming commitment presents to each person, and also recognizing their need for penitence and healing.

There are special services of prayer that can be used with the candidates in the preparation group or in the Sunday services.

Baptism and confirmation

When an adult is baptized, the liturgy shows very clearly how Jesus' death and resurrection is intimately linked with the change taking place in an individual. People die to a life lived without faith and outside the Church. They are born into a new life of faith, joining the community of Christians in the Church. They receive the sign of water and laying-on of hands; perhaps they are anointed with oil. They join with the Church for the first time to receive the bread and the wine of the Eucharist in holy communion. In confirmation, people who were baptized as babies celebrate the truth and power of that baptism and receive blessing and grace for their life in the service of Christ in the world.

Reflection and ministry after baptism and confirmation

The time after baptism (traditionally the time between Easter and the feast of Pentecost) is the period for helping people to reflect on what has happened and to enter into the meaning of baptism, confirmation and holy communion for them. In the early Church it was a time for concentrated instruction by the bishop.

Many parishes bemoan the way young people disappear from church almost as soon as they have been confirmed. Often this is because they have seen confirmation like an exam to be prepared for, passed, and then forgotten – very different from the Way offered here. We are dealing with preparation for the lifelong ministry of the baptized as Christians in the world.

Someone who is baptized is caught up in God's mission to his world.

He or she becomes an agent in the work of the Kingdom of God which Jesus came to proclaim and initiate.

So this time after the great events of baptism, confirmation and first communion, or after a reaffirmation of commitment to baptism, is a very important opportunity for two aspects of the process. First, it is a time to reflect quietly and deeply on the spiritual and practical effect of what has taken place. Secondly, it is a time to relate all this to the opportunities for Christian witness and service that exist in everyone's everyday lives. The great themes of peace, justice and service of the poor will naturally have been part of the work of the main time of learning and growing in preparation for baptism or confirmation. But there is a sense in which the commitment carried in that sacrament casts a new light on people's involvement in them. Before, they may have looked at these themes almost from the outside; now they are to be part of their life.

It is a very important time, which ought never to be skimped. People rightly expect help from the church as they begin life as full members.

Variations

It is by no means common practice for all adults to be baptized or confirmed at Easter. Nor is it very common for adults who come to join the life of the local church to be unbaptized or even unconfirmed. The journey I have outlined in this chapter follows someone who is coming from a position of little or no faith. It celebrates their journey of conversion with celebrations that mark the stages along the way. It may lead to baptism, confirmation, a return to communion, or a renewal of baptismal promises.

In most parishes you will need to make your own adjustments to the basic pattern, because people are different and circumstances vary. The timetable may have to be fitted in with the bishop's availability for the confirmation service. The liturgies will almost certainly have to celebrate different sorts of sacramental journeys for people who were christened as babies, people who were confirmed in adolescence, and people who are following the path towards adult baptism.

It is important that the truth of people's journeys is respected in what happens in the services. It would be quite wrong in the liturgy to treat people who are baptized as if they were unbaptized, for instance.

The liturgies should express two sorts of truth. They need to be true to the personal lives of the candidates, celebrating the events of their discovery of Christian faith and their approach to the Church. They should reinforce their growing sense of commitment to the Christian way of life. They also need to be true to the wider tradition of the community the candidates are joining. Adapt them to the local circumstances.

Initiation is the whole process

It needs to be said quite firmly that what takes place in the different liturgies along the way is not an extended *preparation* for baptism. It is not as though the months spent learning and growing *end* with a first experience of the sacraments of initiation. Rather, the initiation is what is happening all through those months. What it celebrates is a person's conversion.

People discover the teaching of the Church. They grow in a relationship with God through Jesus in the fellowship of the Holy Spirit. They get to know some of the people in the Church; they also begin to share in some of its worship and community life. They become aware that the faith they are entering into makes demands on the way they live and on the kind of choices they make in different aspects of their life. These things are not a preparation for initiation into faith and membership of the Church; they are stages in the actual process of initiation and they are celebrated in the stage-by-stage liturgy.

A sign of this unity in the rite is the marking of people with the cross. In the baptism liturgy of the Alternative Service Book there are two places for signing with the cross. The first is a response to the candidate turning to Christ, repenting of their sins, and renouncing evil. This is all that remains in our liturgy of the Rite of Entry (Service of Welcome) leading to the months of learning and deepening conversion. In the ASB it is followed by the baptism in water within a couple of minutes.

The liturgy of the Adult Way to Faith is not stretching out a rite that was always short. Rather, it is recovering an ancient, extended ritual that, over the years, has become compressed into one single service.

(There are similarities with the marriage service. In the Book of Common Prayer the couple are asked to 'plight their troth', which is old-fashioned language for 'become engaged', and then immediately go on to exchange the consents which constitute their marriage. What was in earlier centuries a series of celebrations marking stages in the progress of two people towards marriage has been squeezed together into one liturgy.)

Worksheet 3A:
Planning

For the group that is to be responsible for implementing and oversee-ing the Adult Way to Faith in the parish. It could be a committee of the church council or a specially formed task group.

Preliminary work

Read Chapter 3 (and Chapters 1 and 2, if you have not already done so).

Task

There are four main items of work. It may take two sessions to com-plete them.

1. Review: What has happened since the last meeting? What deci-sions have been taken by the relevant bodies in your church? Are you ready to proceed?

2. You have agreed to start work on the Adult Way to Faith. Who are the actual people you will be accompanying on their journey?

   (a) Is there already someone asking about confirmation? Are there people on the fringes of church membership that you should be inviting to join?

   (b) Are there church leaders, clergy and others you should ask for names of possible candidates?

   (c) What groups or individuals should you contact for possible people?

   (d) Should you advertise that the process is beginning? How? In the church magazine? give it out in church? on the notice board, in the local press, on local radio?

3. The team: Who have you in mind as possible group leaders and sponsors? What part do you expect the clergy to play? What training do leaders and sponsors need before they begin?

4. What pattern of group working seems most appropriate for your place? What part do you expect the sponsors to play in the groups? Do you want to link sponsors one-to-one with candidates or not? (See the section 'Accompanied' on p. 26.)

5. Timetable: Should you make diary dates, pencilling in:
   (a) training sessions for team members?
   (b) first meeting of the group(s)?
   (c) possible date for a Service of Welcome?
   (d) possible date for the Service of God's Call?
   (e) possible date for baptism and confirmation?
6. What about the place of the bishop in the process?

What consultations need to take place with the bishop about dates, etc.?

Worksheet 3B:
Training Session(s) for Sponsors

This is an outline of a basic preparation for sponsors. People who are to be group leaders should also take part.

The material that follows may take two sessions to complete. It could be a Saturday morning and afternoon, for instance, or two evenings.

Preliminary work

Read this book (or at least Chapters 1 to 3). As you read, be aware of and perhaps jot down in a notebook:

1. Bits of your own story that come to mind; the people and events that seem important to you.
2. Things in the book that excite you.
3. Things in the book that worry you or you don't agree with.

Task

1. The leader welcomes the members and invites them to say who they are and a little about themselves.
2. The leader introduces the session as a time for people to begin the work of accompanying someone on a journey of faith, making it clear that people are not under pressure to be more open than they feel is right for them and that the meeting is to be regarded as confidential.
3. Think for some minutes about why you are here, what you hope to get from the session(s), and what you think you have to offer to the session(s).
4. Depending on the number in the group, either share 3. with the whole group or split into more intimate small groups for this. Reflect on how this exercise feels (without moral judgement!).
5. Ask everyone to spend 20 minutes working in some way on their own story. Possible ways of doing this include:
    (a) Draw a 'life line' which shows the ups and downs at various ages of your life as you think of events that have been important.
    (b) List the people and the events that have mattered to you at different periods of your life. Note how you felt or feel about those periods. The 'Life Chart' on page 38 can be used as a model for this.

Date	Events	People	Feelings or colour	Choices or call and response	Images of God

LIFE CHART

(c) Draw a picture or make a diagram of your life now. (No artistic skill is needed!)

(d) Make a cross dividing a page into four blocks and in the blocks list:

What you enjoy, what gives you pleasure.
What you dislike, what hurts you.
What frightens you.
What you hope for.

(e) Think about the past week and reflect on a high point, something that has been good, and a low point, something that has been bad, for you.

(This might be a good point to break between sessions.)

6. Spend at least 20 minutes in pairs to share with each other the story you have been working on. Some pairs may want to divide the time in half, as listener and speaker and vice versa.

7. The whole group reviews the last two exercises. Look at questions like:

(a) How do you feel about what has happened in the last hour?
(b) What was it like to listen and to be listened to?
(c) What stories of faith were there among the life stories?

8. Do you think any of the activities you have just done would be suitable to do in a group with the enquirers?

(a) Why or why not?
(b) What do you think would be similar or different with them?
(c) Look at the similarities and differences you expect. What skills and weaknesses have you seen in yourself and each other during this session?

9. Consider whether there is a need for further preparation sessions for sponsors or whether it is better for them to begin work and then come back for a reflection and 'in-service' training meeting.

Practicalities

1. Tell the sponsors who the enquirers are likely to be. See if they know them. Ask for prayers for them.

2. Consider how available people are to give time as sponsors, recognizing the commitment to meet with their enquirer and join in group sessions.

3. What are the practical arrangements that have to be made?

4. What are the important dates to be put into diaries for such events as first meeting of the group with enquirers, the Service of Welcome and planning meetings for that, and 'review sessions' for the sponsors?

4

Working in Groups

This chapter deals with the basic building block of the Adult Way to Faith, the community in which most of the work takes place, a small group made up of enquirers and Christian helpers together. The chapter will be particularly useful for people who are to lead groups or act as sponsors within them. Worksheet 3B on pages 37–39 is primarily about training sponsors, though people preparing to lead groups should take part in the sessions. There is a set of worksheets on the training of group leaders at the end of Chapter 5.

Working in groups

The minister of a parish that has followed the Adult Way to Faith for several years writes:

> As I see it, the Adult Way to Faith is so much part of how things are done here and of the ethos of our Christian life that it hardly needs naming. In particular, there is an emphasis on working in groups in people's homes, including the confirmation preparation for adults and for young people. The other day we started yet another group for half-a-dozen inquirers. They are all led by members of the congregation with the clergy only turning up when invited. Within such a group the participants set their own agenda, starting with their own concerns. We hope that the group will be flexible enough to respond to any pressing problem that any member needs to share. It's not chained to its programme. It would now be totally foreign to us to 'Teach the Faith' in a dogmatic, take-it-or-leave way.

Christianity as community

To become a Christian on your own is, if not impossible, at least very difficult and incredibly rare. You need other people. This is because Christianity is about community. It involves belonging to a church. Jesus did not leave behind him a religion. He left a group of people. Christians today are the successors of his friends and followers, the apostles and the others who made up the first body of disciples. 'The

Body of Christ' is a fellowship that stretches back over the centuries and includes people of all continents. Jesus lives and works in the world through his people. That is why 'community' is one of the essential marks of this way of accompanying men and women into faith.

Special purpose

It is important to remember from the start that the groups come together in order to accompany men and women on their early steps of the journey into faith. They need to be formed for that purpose. Experience has shown that it does not work to use groups that already exist, like home groups or Lent groups, and adapt them for welcoming new Christians. The dynamics are all wrong. Preparation groups have a life of their own, a purpose of their own, and a time limit as well. They should last for as long as they are needed by the candidates and then stop meeting. They will have a continuing life as a group of friends who care for one another, but their official job is done once the new Christians are established in their new life and ministry.

Forming a group

How you go about setting up a group or groups will depend on the particular circumstances in your place. It will usually fall to the clergy to be responsible for this aspect of the work. It is often they who have the best awareness of who is who in the congregation and an insight into the suitable matching of candidate to helper. This task could also be shared with lay people who will be responsible for the group.

My own practice (diagram 1) has been to consider the enquirers and see who in the congregation would be suitable as a leader for these men and women. Two leaders in a group are often better than one. A man and a woman working together provide a balance that often reflects the make-up of the group.

Say there are four or five people who have asked to join the group with a view to being confirmed. I would think of two people who would be suitable leaders of a group to accompany them. I would then look for people from the church I might invite to join as helpers in the group. They might be people who have asked for a refresher course or people whom I have selected as suitable for this specific group. They may also be people who themselves might be asked to be leaders of a group next year. What happens in this model is that the group travels together and provides support and care from within its own membership. The members act as sponsors to one another, although there is no formal one-to-one pairing of sponsor and candidate.

A second way of setting up groups (diagram 2) begins with just such a one-to-one pairing. It is then a matter of forming a group from pairs of candidates and sponsors with leaders.

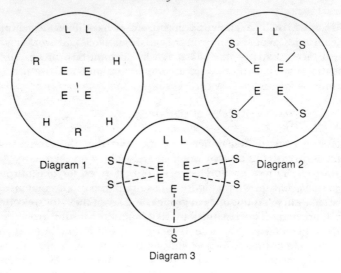

Diagram 1

Diagram 2

Diagram 3

R = 'Refresher'   H = Helper
L = Leader   E = Enquirer   S = Sponsor

In the third pattern (diagram 3) the group will consist of the leader or leaders usually meeting with the candidates alone. The candidates will have individual sponsors and will each meet with his or her sponsor at a different time to talk about their learning and growing in the faith, perhaps delving more deeply into things that the group meetings have dealt with. There will also be times when the sponsors take part in the main group meetings together with the candidates. This way of working has the advantage of asking the sponsors for a rather less demanding commitment as far as time is concerned. But there are drawbacks.

Where the sponsors are not part of the main work of the group, it is often difficult for them to know quite what they are supposed to be doing. It is easy for them to feel out of the main stream of what is going on. There is also an opportunity lost. Time and again sponsors have said something like 'I don't know what Barry and Liz got out of this past year, but my husband and I have really grown. We've discovered so much about our faith and the church by being their sponsors and going through it all with them.'

Fixing meetings: How? When? Where?

The process can start just as soon as one person comes to ask to join the church, to find out more about Christianity, or whatever their approach may be. It begins with welcome and some kind of sponsoring by lay people of the newcomer. However, you may need to wait till there are more than one or two enquirers before linking them with church members to make up a group.

You may well have several groups running at the same time. Availability of rooms, number of enquirers, number of leaders and the time of year that people come forward all have a bearing. Some parishes have an enquirers group which runs most of the time to welcome people in the very earliest stage of their journeys and to feed them into learning and growing groups when they are ready for that.

You are faced with practical choices when setting up groups. The place where the group meets has an effect on how it develops. My preference is for meetings in a home, but it may be right in some cases to use a room in the church or the church hall.

Ordinary human comfort is important. It is an essential part of welcome. Hospitality is a sign of the Church's love for people. So warmth, chairs that don't leave people with a stiff back for days afterwards, and easy lighting are all essential considerations in setting up a group meeting.

If the meeting is in someone's house, you have to decide whether it is a good or a bad thing for it to be the leader's home. It is usually easier not to have the double job of hosting and being responsible for the work of the meeting. Over the months it may be a good thing to move round different homes, so spreading the load.

When and how long should the session be? The answer depends on the candidates. What is the best time for them? How are they affected by shift work or family responsibilities? For some the best time may be evenings. Others prefer afternoons before their children come home from school. Others are coffee-morning people. Where there are families with children you need to consider whether the church ought to provide baby-sitters to relieve the candidates of having to pay for them.

Set a sensible time limit for the sessions and do your best to stick to it. Let it be agreed by all the members, so that anyone can feel free to leave when that time is up. An hour and a half or two hours is probably enough. Any longer can be very tiring.

Make a decision about refreshments. Starting with tea or coffee helps break the ice and gives space for some people to arrive a bit later than others. Ending with refreshments at a definite time arranged beforehand makes a good stopping point when there is a danger of running on and on. A half-way break is the most difficult. It is hard to get the time right, and refreshments often disturb the flow of a meeting. One vital word of warning. Beware of 'cake competitions'! If you are moving round different homes, try to establish an agreed level of hospitality and stick to it.

You will also need to decide how often the group will meet. There are several patterns to choose from. It could be regularly every week or every fortnight through the year. This could be too great a commitment for some people. Some groups meet in bursts of weekly meetings over six, eight or ten weeks and then have a break.

Some meet on Sundays after the service. There are also those,

particularly in the USA, who follow the way of the early Church and
meet with candidates during the second part of the parish Eucharist;
they withdraw to 'break the Word' while the communicants break the
bread.

People in the group also need to decide whether to stick to a set time
and day of the week. There may be conflicting needs among the
members which will mean you have to keep making adjustments.

Leading a group

The first and most important thing for anyone invited to lead one of
these groups to get clearly into their head is that they are not being
asked to be a professor, school teacher or instructor. Their main job
is to make it possible for other people to learn and grow as Christians.
They are to be what today's jargon terms 'enablers'. Certainly, they
are often going to be in a position to share some of their own experience
of discipleship or to explain how they understand the Church's
teaching. But they do not need to know it all. They don't have to have
a degree in theology.

It may be a help to some leaders to have done a certain amount of
Christian study, perhaps to have taken a Bishop's Certificate course
or some other sort of lay training. But it will be far more valuable to
have done some training in the skills of group leadership, or to have
had some experience in leading Lent groups, Bible studies or other
forms of adult learning in small groups.

There *are* skills to be learnt, but they are very hard to pick up from
a book. So what I write here is not in any sense a complete training
to equip someone to be a group leader. Rather, it simply hints at the
areas that need to be looked at, reviewed and developed in order for
what happens in the life of a group to help the members to learn and
grow in Christian discipleship.

It is a bit like being a good host or hostess at a party. The similarities
are in the welcome, in making people feel at home, and treating them
like valued guests. A good group leader sees that people are comfor-
table, helps them to relax and get on together, and tries to give
everyone their chance to be heard when they want to say something.

On the other hand, the good group leader is not there to get the party
going with a swing. A group meeting should not be all activity and
noise. There needs to be time for reflection. Silence is not a failure;
it often marks a high point in a session. Nor is conflict necessarily
wrong. Imagine a roomful of eight or so people. That means not only
eight different characters; it also means eight different experiences of
life, eight different ways of meeting and thinking about God, and eight
different ways of praying. In a group of eight people there are also
twenty-eight possible personal relationships. The conflict that may
arise from these is real and needs to be faced honestly.

So a very large part of the work of leading a group is about the relationships among the people who make up the group. It is about an atmosphere of respect, welcome and tact. It is not going too far to say that what good leadership requires is Christian love. It also needs some ability to manage people. This does not mean dominating them, ordering them about, or forcing them to do what you want. It means making it possible for the group to function well and to achieve what it is there for. We looked at some of the practicalities of this earlier on. There are also the personal skills to be learnt and practised, like ways of encouraging shy people to feel brave enough to contribute, and ways of encouraging the people who cannot stop talking and being the centre of attention to give way and let other people have a chance.

Preparation

If the group is to function well and achieve what it is there for, the leader's job is to help this to happen. Not to *make* it happen, because everyone in the group shares the responsibility for that. Good leaders use their particular skills and gifts to enable everyone to learn and grow as disciples of Jesus. They act as coaches or guides to their companions as they travel together along the journey of faith and continuing conversion to Christ.

To do this well needs preparation and planning beforehand. Leaders who work in pairs can prepare and review sessions together, as well as give each other support during the session itself.

I want now to look rather more closely at that side of the work, though you will find more about the actual content of the process of learning and growing in the next chapter.

Most leaders need the security of having some kind of structure to a group session in their minds before they start. There are the basics: you need to have a timetable to show when people should arrive; when you will have refreshments, if you think that is appropriate; when the working part of the session should start and finish; and when you expect people to leave. These are all things that ought to be agreed by everyone, but the leader has to take the initiative and offer suggestions.

You need to have a clear idea of the subject-matter for the session, and how you want to begin and develop the work. You need to know what kind of prayer you expect to be part of the session. You need to arrange any equipment you need, like Bibles or a flip chart, a video or a tape recorder.

As well as needing the security of good planning, you also need to be flexible and move with the people in the meeting. After all, they are the reason for the session in the first place.

I think of the leader who planned a lovely evening on the Creation. She had worked out Bible readings. She had a video of volcanoes and Pacific islands. She brought a special music tape as a background to a period of quiet prayer. And it all went for nothing. The daughter of a middle-aged couple in the group had presented them with their first grandchild during the week and they could think of nothing else. All evening they and everyone else talked excitedly about babies!

Leading a group is more like riding a horse with a will of its own than being in a train running along set tracks.

Success and failure

Most people like to be appreciated. They like to be told when they have done things well. It is important when you begin to do something that you know how to recognize whether or not it has been successful. There are not many exact markers of success and failure in leading this kind of group. You may have a good feeling at the end of a session because everyone seemed cheerful and chatty. You got through most of the material you had prepared on the resurrection of Jesus. So you feel it went well. It could be a couple of days before you realize that one of the group was intensely sad and worried, but could not bring herself to open up because of the overwhelming hearty feeling of the evening. She felt quite excluded but played along with the others because she was afraid she might break down and cry.

There are so many levels at which the life and work of a group go on. People's feelings, their understanding and the relationships between them are all involved. Much of the skill of leading is in being sensitive to as many of these different things as possible. You need to see how your group can travel together, accompanying one another into deeper awareness of faith in God, closer following of Jesus, and growing commitment to the work of the Kingdom in the world of everyday work, neighbourhood and home.

Success may not necessarily mean that all the scalps in your group will be offered to the bishop for confirmation. Success may well include someone deciding that the claims of the Gospel are too much for them to accept at this time. They may recognize that they are not yet ready. Your success is in being true to the truth that has been given to you and sharing it with them.

Summary

'Content', the subject-matter of the group sessions, and 'Process', the way the group works, both need care. People learn and grow through relating and absorbing the community life and the personal relationships within the group just as much as they do through discussing the material that forms the subject of the session programme.

The leader has to hold three important aspects of the work in balance – often in tension! The diagram of three interlocking circles has stood the test of time. For a session to go well, the leader needs to keep three things in mind about the meeting:

1. The *task* is the reason why people have met. The overall task of these groups is, of course, to accompany people into faith and to help

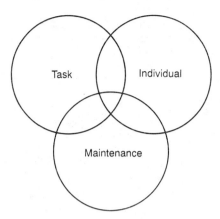

them prepare for Christian initiation. When you meet there is usually a subject you are working on or an activity you want to see achieved.

2. The group is made up of *individuals*, each of whom has their own needs and their own gifts to bring to the meeting. The leader's job is to see that as far as possible every member is given the opportunity to say what they have to say, that they are respected and helped to feel completely a part of what is going on. Under this heading comes the proper pastoral care that the leader has for the people in the group, a care that is shared with the others who also belong.

3. The life of the group itself needs *maintenance*. There are the practical provisions that need always to be kept in mind and there are the different aspects of management to watch. The leader needs to be alert to those factors that help or hinder the working of the group. Be aware of the relationships and pressures between people, as well as practical things like the arrangement of chairs and the courtesies of fixing suitable dates and times, and of letting people who are absent know the arrangements for next time.

5

Learning and Growing

This chapter is particularly important for those people who are to lead groups. It will also be helpful for those who act as sponsors to enquirers. At the end, there is a series of worksheets drawing on material in the chapter and providing a short course of training for group leaders.

Faith sharing

The key to the chapter lies in the idea of 'faith sharing'. What we are dealing with here is not instruction in the faith. It is about helping people to grow in faith in God and Jesus, which is something more often 'caught' than 'taught'. The heart of it is the relationship between a man or a woman and the God who has made himself known in the life, death and resurrection of Jesus Christ. It is celebrated in worship within his community, the Church, and lived out in the relationships, attitudes and choices of everyday life in the world.

Dialogue and conversation are at the heart of the process. The way people get to know one another and get to know about things is by talking and listening. For this to work well there needs to be respect between the parties in the conversation. That is why in the work of the groups the keynotes of welcome, respect and trust are essential.

Story

Just as in some church circles 'sharing' is a word that has taken on a particular colour of its own, so 'story' has become a bit of a buzz word. Nevertheless, I am going to use both quite unashamedly.

Ask someone to tell you about themselves and it is more likely than not that their reply will be to share a story that describes some aspect of their life. 'I'm married and we've got three lovely children at school.' 'I used to work as a fitter at Smith and Brown's, but I got laid off last June and haven't been able to get another job since.' 'I used to be a happy sort of person. Then my brother was killed on his motorbike and I just don't seem to be able to get over it.'

Begin at the beginning

That is where the accompanied journey into faith begins. The only place from which people can start is where they are. Far too often the Church expects them to start from where the Church expects them to be. Begin with listening. Of course enquirers have questions they want to raise, and some of these, usually the most practical ones, need to be answered early on. Deep spiritual questions about the meaning of life and what it is all for take far longer; they need to be answered not by a simple sentence from a teacher, but by reflection on one's own personal experience and insight, together with reflection on God's revelation of himself in Jesus Christ and by entering into the record of that revelation in Scripture.

In the early part of the journey the work of the group is centred on getting to know one another. People are invited to tell their own stories. This can mean either telling the story of my life or talking about what really matters to me. Different people at different times in their lives will want to do one or the other. In either case, people are sharing what is important to them. It matters to Winston that his mother came from Barbados. It matters to Jenny that her little girl has to go into hospital next week for an operation. It matters to Brian and Kylie that the doctor has given his father only a few more months to live. Bob and Ellen just live to see Liverpool at the top of the First Division!

To listen to people's stories and encourage them to tell them does not mean being inquisitive. You need to be sensitive and not tread heavily where you have not been invited. It is more than a way of simply getting to know people better; it is starting with people where they feel themselves to be. More than that, it is trying to make it possible to discern where God is in their lives and where they are able to be open to him. The place where we are often most open to God is where we are most concerned about something or someone. It is where our feelings and our interest are most alive; where we hurt or where we want most deeply.

The Gospel story

Conversations involve more than one person. The dialogue here is between the stories of individuals and the story of the Christian Gospel. People with their histories, their interests and concerns come face to face with the Good News of God's love shown in Jesus. There is opportunity and space for both the person and the Gospel to interact, to challenge and to respond, as someone brings their deep concerns to the God they meet in his story or as that story enters into their heart.

'What has your God got to say to the pain and grief of people starving in Ethiopia? Every time I see famine on the TV it hurts so much. I can't understand how you can say God is almighty and loves people when things like that keep going on and on.'

'When you told us that story about Jesus healing the man who was lying paralysed by the pool, it made me think about myself. I wonder whether I'm just sitting back and waiting for other people to do things for me when I could probably get up and get going myself.'

'That elder brother who was cross when the other one was given a party. It's like that in my family. We've sort of cut Joan off since she got into trouble with the police over drugs. We ought really to make it up with her, I suppose.'

When I say 'Gospel story', I admit I am using shorthand. I mean something that of course includes the New Testament gospels, but also reflects the whole inheritance of the Church to which we belong. I am talking about the Good News which today's Christian has to share with today's enquirer who lives in today's world.

The Good News is there in the events we read about in the Bible. It is the story of God's self-giving love for his people, the story of his covenant relationship with the people of the Old Testament, Israel, and following them with the New Testament Church and those who have belonged to the community of the Body of Christ over the succeeding centuries. The Bible contains one story of God's initiative and people's response. It is also made up of countless different stories. When we use it as a base for the learning and growing of newcomers to the faith, people can hear and react both to the overall story and to the different stories within it.

This reflects the method Jesus used when he taught in parables. A parable is a good story in its own right. What makes it a tool for teaching is the way in which it sparks off some kind of response in the hearer. Maybe it challenges you to review your own behaviour.

Think for example of the parable of the rich man and Lazarus; notice its sharp contrast between the life-styles of the man feasting indoors and the sore-infested beggar outside. Maybe it opens your spiritual vision to respond in some way to God.

If the anxious housewife can get so excited at finding the coin she lost, what a wonderful thought that God can get excited when he finds someone like me turning towards him!

What is happening here is more than the kind of work that is sometimes done in Bible study groups, which are often based quite heavily 'in the head': As people try together to deepen their understanding of the message, analysis, meaning and cross-references take up a lot of their time. In the story-to-story dialogue I am suggesting here, the meaning of a passage is naturally an important part of the work, but it is not the main part nor the most effective. The question is not so much 'What does this passage mean, how do I explain it, or how does it relate to this or that aspect of Christian belief?' Rather, it is:

'As I hear this passage, what does it mean to me? What does this passage tell me about Jesus, about God? How do I hear it? Where does it key in with my life, my experience and my attitudes?'

And this leads on to the converting question: 'So what changes does this passage ask of me?'

Models for story work

There are any number of different ways a group can open out the Bible for its members. Here are just two examples which are designed to help people bring the Scripture story face to face with their own lives.

An African model

In this way there is no need for people to read the text. It is a matter of listening and reflecting:

1. Opening prayer to gather the members together and focus the session.
2. Ask people to listen for a word or phrase that stands out or speaks for them. Read the Gospel passage aloud slowly and deliberately.
3. One minute of silence.
4. Invite everyone simply to say the word or phrase that touched them. Do not discuss!
5. Read the Gospel passage again.
6. Tell the group you will give them five minutes of silence to be with the Gospel (or three minutes if they are new to it). Be quiet for that time.
7. Invite them to note what they hear in their heart, what the passage touches in their life. They could write it down.
8. Divide into groups of not more than four or five, perhaps twos and threes, to speak of what they have got from the Gospel passage. It is very important that they use the word 'I' and own their personal experience and insight, rather than say what others believe. It is not a time for discussing or preaching or solving the problems of other people.
9. Read the gospel passage again.
10. Ask people to consider what, in the light of the meeting so far, they believe God wants from them this week. How is God inviting them to change? What are they taking home with them this week? Specific answers are important, rather than responses like 'God wants me to be good for ever and ever'!
11. Again, in small groups, share these answers.
12. Gather the group together for a closing prayer with perhaps one of the Sunday readings, open prayer, silence and singing.
13. Give details of the next meeting and the passages to be read.

American model

For this pattern I have drawn on two sources, Raymond Kemp's experience at St Augustine's Church, Washington, DC, and the work of Karen Hinman Powell, as I have met them at training events in the USA.

1. Opening prayer, to include a reading of the gospel.

2. Reflections on the gospel:
(a) What did you hear? Note three thoughts, ideas, phrases, images that grabbed you in the reading.
(b) What does it mean? Why did these words or images grab you today? What do they mean for your life? Can you recall a time in your life (past or present) in which you experienced something similar to the event in today's reading? How does the reading enlighten or challenge that experience?
(c) What questions does today's reading raise for you about being a Christian?
(d) What does it cost you to live this passage? Note one concrete way in which you feel called to live this message this week. What will help you to live this? What will be the obstacles?
3. Divide into small groups for members to share their reflections with one another.
4. All together in one group, share insights learned and any questions left unresolved.
5. Quiet reflection. Ask people to name one concrete way in which they feel challenged to live differently this week. Let the changes be small, definite and limited.
6. Share this with one or two people.
7. Closing prayer.
8. Arrangements for next meeting.

The Church

The Good News is not to be found only in the pages of the Bible. It can be recognized in the changed lives of the people of God over the centuries. Anyone coming to Christian faith in the present century is aware in one way or another that they are entering into a long inheritance of spiritual tradition. For some it may be the tradition that is expressed in the local parish church built in 1857 or in the fifteenth century. It surfaces in the worship that takes place in that church with roots that stretch back to the Last Supper, to the Divine Office of early Benedictine monasteries, or the hymns of the Wesleys. It also causes confusion because it carries the echoes of controversies and hurts from many past ages. These still break out and distort God's loving welcome as church men and women voice partisan battle cries or narrow the vastness of his message into tight little doctrinal statements.

The word 'tradition' simply means something that is handed on. Sponsors and group leaders have a duty to pass on the tradition that they have received from others. That, after all, seems to be why the Bible exists. It was written, put together and handed on within the Church. Within the wide tradition of Christianity, the Bible has its uniquely privileged position as a record of what has happened in the past and as a guide to today's Christian living and believing.

In working with enquirers and new Christians there should be a

conscious balance between the demands of what is inherited in statements and written documents and the immediate contemporary
meeting between a person and Christ present in the telling of the Good
News.

Syllabus or demand feeding?

I have suggested that, at least in the earlier part of the journey, much
of the work in the groups is led by the stories that the enquirers have
to tell. The material for discussion is what they bring rather than what
the leaders think they ought to be teaching. I have also suggested that
unless this listening to the stories of the people in the group continues
to be recognized and valued as a strong element in the life of the group,
it will not fulfil its purpose of accompanying men and women along the
journey of conversion. God is at work in people's lives in real events,
real relationships and real feelings, perceptions and reactions.

Group leaders sometimes say 'Fine. I see it's important to give the
enquirers their say, but how are we to know what to do in the sessions?'

From experience, I suggest that the answer goes something like this:
'Don't worry too much about doing it right. It's normal for parishes
to start with fairly structured sessions in the groups. Then, as they get
more confident over a couple of years, they become far more flexible.'

It is normal for a parish starting out to use the Adult Way to Faith
to carry into it something from what has happened in the past. So at
first group leaders are likely to follow the kind of pattern that the
minister used in his adult confirmation classes. They will ask for a
syllabus of topics to be covered and suggestions for each session – a
kind of lesson plan. This should be a co-operative effort with the
minister and the leaders planning and reviewing the sessions as they
go through the season. They should also work hard to move the focus
of attention away from the subject-matter and the leader towards the
enquirers in the group and towards the idea of dialogue between them
and the subject.

Forget the attitude that sees the Christian education of adult lay men
and women as the same kind of thing that the clergy did for a university
degree or at theological college – but made simple for simple folk! It
may be right to have as a basis for the course something that covers the
main headings of Christian belief and the life and practice of the
Church. There are several textbooks available for leaders who want to
work along those lines.

But I hope that in the actual meetings of the group people will ease
out beyond the boundaries that are set by the image of the teacher who
is expert in the Christian tradition instructing the ignorant about the
mysteries. All group members are to travel together into an experience
of living faith and to put it into practice in the decisions and relationships of their daily life, as people who are themselves caught up in
God's mission of peace and justice to his world.

There is a very fine syllabus already given to us in the Christian year. Many churches work on the principle that they do not need any other textbook in the catechumenate apart from the readings which, Sunday by Sunday, tell the story of God's dealings with his people.

Perhaps this is specially valuable when the sessions take place on a Sunday at the time of the main service. Where this happens there should be an opportunity for co-ordination between the preacher and the work of the group so that some kind of integrated teaching can take place.

A half-way house between the syllabus approach and the more open way could be found in having a checklist of themes that should be covered during the course. Again I suggest that this is something that ought to be developed jointly by clergy and lay people involved in the catechumenate, so that together they can work out what could be called a local baptismal creed – the things that we in our church believe people should have covered, understand or be at home with before they come to be baptized or confirmed. Working out such a list is a useful exercise in itself!

Checklist

I expect most Christians would include in their checklist most of the headings that follow, although different communities will put different emphases on some parts. You may well have other important topics you want to add.

Prayer

How can you help people into a relationship with God? What place does it have in personal life and the work of the group? (This is the subject of Chapter 6.)

Public worship

How are people helped to take part in church? How does participation contribute to our Christian formation as individuals and as the Holy People of God? The shape of the Eucharist and other services. The books, the hymns and the language.

Creation

What is the world we live in? What is it for? What does it mean to say God is the Creator? What is the responsibility of human beings in the world or for the world?

'The Fall'

If we believe God is good and loves us, why is there such trouble and wrong in the world? What is the status of humanity: good, but distorted by sin? Or totally lost? What does 'sin' mean?

God and his people

What do we mean by 'covenant', 'The Chosen People', as we read the Old and New Testaments?

Incarnation

In Jesus, God took on human flesh. How do we express the faith that Jesus is both fully God and fully human?

The ministry of Jesus

Proclaiming the Good News of the Kingdom, healing and teaching. How are the parables and miracles Good News for us and for our time?

The Passion and death of Jesus, his resurrection

What do these mean for us? How do we hear words like 'redemption', 'atonement', 'salvation' or 'sacrifice'?

Pentecost and the Holy Spirit

What do they mean for us? Where do you stand in relation to Charismatic Renewal? Where do you see evidence of the Holy Spirit in your relationships?

'One, Holy, Catholic and Apostolic Church'

What do these individual words mean to you? How are they expressed on the ground in your locality? What does the Church mean to you? How important is it in your day-to-day walk with God?

The Bible

How are people to read it? What does 'This is the Word of the Lord' mean to you?

The Church's ministry

What are bishops, priests and deacons? What is their responsibility? What is the responsibility of lay people in the Church?

Authority

Where does authority lie in the Church? What is the authority of the ordained ministers, of the laity and of the whole people of God? How is it exercised and how should it be exercised?

Right and wrong

What areas of moral choice are important for you? How do you choose?

The mission of the Church

What is evangelism? How can you/do you bear witness to the Gospel in everyday life? How can/should the Church serve those in need?

Life in the church

How does the parish work? What is a Parish Council for? How is church life funded and what is your responsibility in this?

Life in the world

What difference does being a Christian make to life at home, at work or in the community? What is the relationship between Christianity and politics? What are the things about modern life that make it hard to be a Christian and how can you deal with them?

Local adaptation

It must by now be clear that I am trying to avoid writing a blueprint to be followed slavishly in every situation. Quite the opposite. I believe that plants will only grow well if they are cared for properly and rooted in the soil that is right for them. So it would be wrong of me to lay down my own personal colour of belief and practice as a norm for all to follow. Rather, what I hope to do is to present some guidelines that you may use or not as you wish.

People who come to join your church have chosen to do so. There are alternatives they could have chosen but did not. This means that the process and the content of groups ought to be true to the ethos of *your* church.

Conversion and the whole person

Learning and growing in discipleship involves change; in other words, conversion. Sponsors and leaders represent the Church and are there to accompany people through their conversion to faith in Jesus Christ. I suspect that many will feel that they are quite inadequate for this task, largely because they have a particular picture in their mind of what conversion means. Thus it may be useful to think a bit more widely around what this learning, growing and changing might mean.

Human beings are creatures with a body, a mind, senses, instincts, emotions and a will. We can experience all these aspects of what it means to be a person. It is rather harder to experience what it means to have a soul. We have an idea of what 'spiritual' might mean; it often refers to what we have felt or come to understand in ways that go beyond any of the faculties I have just mentioned. There is a sense in which when we make important choices, our will draws on something deep within us which we can call our soul. It is more than personality or character, though 'who I *really* am' could well come near to describing what 'soul' might mean.

I am one person. I cannot be split up into different departments. Intelligence, feelings, will and all the other faculties work together as I live my life. But there is more to me than that. It is hard to imagine what it could be like to be a person totally and utterly alone. So much of who I am is linked with how I relate to people and to things outside of myself. We are individual men and women, certainly, but it is as we live out our lives in all sorts of different relationships that we grow into fuller people.

So much by way of background to our thinking about conversion to Christ. If a journey from little or no Christian faith towards belief, commitment and membership of the Church is to mean anything worthwhile, it simply has to involve the whole of a person, all those different aspects and faculties. A complete personality is engaged.

One or other side of a person will be more important than the others. For some people the opening to belief may come through events and choices that throw up questions of right and wrong. They may be challenged in their conscience about things they have done or said in the past; they realize that they need to be forgiven somehow. Or it may be that they are faced with terribly hard decisions in life which they sense they are quite inadequate to deal with on their own.

Questions about the meaning of life are the entry point for quite a few. How are we to reconcile human suffering and the unfairness of life with the goodness, truth and beauty that we also see around us? Can the vast complex universe be explained as something that just happened in a random way, or is there a purpose behind it?

For some people, God seems to take a hand directly. Far more people than usually admit it have had some kind of spiritual experience, an awareness that comes to them of a reality beyond themselves.

Feelings and emotions often play an important part in this process of change, just as they do in many important choices and changes that people make in their lives. Fear or attraction, a longing for the warmth of love and acceptance, the excitement of belonging to something alive or perhaps even the enjoyment of music or a lovely building – any of these can be the starting point or an aid to the development of conversion.

A choice to be made

For most people conversion is a gradual process. There may well be high and low points along the way. Some of these may be dramatic changes or experiences charged with strong emotion. Some may involve costly decisions about life-styles or behaviour. What I want to emphasize is that if the journey of learning and growing in faith and loyalty is to be true, it has to be concerned with the whole of personality. Feelings matter, the mind matters, our perceptions matter. In the end, what matters most are the choices we make.

One of the hardest things to describe in the process of conversion is who is responsible for it. In the list of the aspects of what it means to be a person there are some faculties where you are in charge and making the decisions. You can see or you can shut your eyes. You can respond to someone in a conversation or choose to keep quiet. You can try to come to a decision or just shelve it. But feelings and emotions tend to happen whether you want them to or not. Spiritual experiences are like that too; you cannot choose to have them. When it comes to choosing whether or not to believe, to make an act of faith or to commit your life to God, there is a sense in which you are both in charge of the decision and not in charge. You change the direction of your life; you alter your attitudes towards God and towards other people; you open your heart to a new kind of love for your Creator and Saviour. Or do you? Is it just as true to say that your heart is opened, your attitudes and your direction are changed for you?

The truth is that the initiative lies with God who works in us and with us, using many different sides of our personality. But we also have a responsibility of our own, to agree or to refuse, to say Yes or to say No.

And so . . .

Just as the whole of a person is involved in coming to conversion, so too we should expect that the effects of conversion will show in all aspects of personality and relationships. Here again, as all of us know from our own painful experience, we are talking about a gradual, often shamingly slow, process rather than a sudden and immediate flash of total perfection. Continuing conversion throughout life means a deepening in our awareness of God and in our relationship with him. It also means a continual recognition of our need for greater love, greater truth, fuller holiness, as we are being shaped into the person that God has designed us to become.

Worksheet 5:
Training Group Leaders
(several sessions)

Introduction

This set of worksheets gives outline ideas for several sessions which will work best if they take place in a group of between five and ten people. It may be advisable to have leaders from different churches in the neighbourhood meeting together in order to get suitable numbers.

It may also be advisable to invite a trainer with some experience to lead the sessions. Diocesan lay ministry advisers, adult education departments or church societies should be able to help here.

Recognize that you will learn by your own experience of taking part in the meetings of this group. Notice your own feelings and reactions and be prepared to talk about them.

Practical points

1. Make diary dates for as many leader training sessions as are likely to be needed. Fix venues for these sessions.

2. Make diary dates through the next few months for review sessions with the leaders and the clergy together.

Training topics

Separate sessions may concentrate on different areas:

5A The practice of leading a group.
5B The relationship between Content and Process.
5C Ways of working with people's own stories.
5D Ways of working with the Bible and the tradition of the Church.

Worksheet 5A:
Leading a Group

---

1. Reflect together on what has happened in the meetings that members of the group have been involved in so far.

   (a) What has been the experience of the members and of the leaders?

   (b) How well have you achieved your tasks?

   (c) How has each member been helped or hindered by life within the group and by the leadership of the group?

   (d) What problems have had to be faced and how have they been dealt with?

2. Make a list of topics for discussion. Let each member act as leader for one of the topics for 15 minutes, first giving a short introduction. Spend five minutes reviewing how each session went.

Worksheet 5B:
Content and Process

1. Spend time reflecting together on Chapters 4 and 5.
   (a) What help do leaders need in order to feel confident about faith sharing?
   (b) How do you feel about a syllabus or a checklist of topics for the group?
   (c) What effect has the training so far had upon the faith, confidence or understanding of members of the group?
   (d) What would be the important elements of a 'Baptism Creed' in your local church? What do you think should be the marks of readiness for membership?
2. List the important things that have come out of the session.
3. Pray together about these important things.

Worksheet 5C:
Individual Stories

---

1. Spend time alone on your own story (perhaps in preparation at home for this session). You could use one of the suggestions in Worksheet 3B. Enter into something that is important to you (for whatever reason) and that you are prepared to talk about with someone else.

2. In pairs, spend half an hour on each other's stories. Give attention to the quality of your listening. Be aware not only of the human interest and importance of the story, but also of where you can discern God at work in the other person's life.

3. In the main group, share what has happened in the pairs.

4. Close with a simple, structured time of worship that expresses what has happened during the session.

Worksheet 5D:
Bible and Tradition

The session is to be spent working from a Bible passage. The purpose is to let the Bible story have its effect on people's lives, rather than spend time analysing it in an intellectual way.

Preliminary work

Choose the passage to be used. This could be the next Sunday's gospel or a passage which seems to be particularly appropriate to the work of the group. Suggestions include the call of the disciples (Mark 1.15-20 or John 1.35-42); the healing of the paralysed man (Mark 2.1-12 or Luke 5.17-26); the stilling of the storm (Mark 4.35-41); Zacchaeus (Luke 19.1-10) or, from the story of the early Church, Philip and the Ethiopian (Acts 8.26-40).

Task

1. Use either the 'African' or 'American' method outlined in Chapter 5 to work with the chosen passage. (If the group is large enough, divide into two so that each group can use one or other of the two methods.) Spend about three-quarters of an hour on this.
2. Break for refreshments.
3. Spend 20 minutes in a review of the work with the Bible. (If the group divided, this will include each group sharing their experience with the other.)
4. Close with a simple, structured time of worship which expresses what has happened during the session.

Worksheet 5E:
Enquiry and Welcome

To help group leaders and clergy in the planning of the early meetings
of the groups.

Practical points

1. Decide on the people who will be in the group(s). This may
depend on a previous decision about whether or not you need an 'Open
Space' occasion to meet enquirers before the actual process begins.
2. Decide what meetings are needed before the Service of Welcome.
This will depend on how well you know the enquirers and how committed you sense they are to joining the programme.
3. If not already done, fix the date of the Service of Welcome.

Session planning

Consider the 'style' of meetings in the early part of the Adult Way to
Faith. What have been your experiences so far in these preparation sessions? Look at the areas of welcome, story telling, listening and faith
sharing. What has been good and needs to be incorporated in the group
sessions, and what has not been helpful and should be avoided?

Design outlines for the first two meetings. Note what the purpose of
the session is. Decide how you will open the session and what work you
propose for the group. If you are working as a pair of leaders, decide
who will do what in the session.

Decide how you will arrange the room, what refreshments you are
to have, and who will provide them. See what equipment, like pencil
and paper, books, video etc., you are likely to need. (It is better to have
more than you actually use than to run out.)

6

Friendship with God in Community

This chapter is written for sponsors and group leaders as they help people to grow in their relationship with God in Jesus. There are skills and attitudes to acquire in order to feel confident in this area and to do it well. Some of these are covered here; others can be learned only from other people in dialogue and relationship. In a growing number of areas there are courses in spiritual direction both for beginners and for people with some experience. These often include an element of support, review, and continuing development for those who are engaged in this ministry.

Praying in the group

Praying together is part of the work of the group accompanying adults into faith. It can take many different forms: sometimes open, free prayer; sometimes following a simple liturgy. It is different from Sunday services, being more personal and intimate. It is also different from private prayer.

It should be more than simply a formal opening or closing with prayer. There should be a space for perhaps a Bible passage, some comment, some reflection and sharing of ideas, reactions and concerns from people in the group; a time of silence and a time for open prayer, spoken or silent, by the members. In the worksheets there are suggestions that the group may devise a simple liturgy as part of its work. Short acts of worship can grow out of the activities of the session.

Talking about prayer

Men and women can be shy about matters of faith. They are reluctant to talk about spirituality. You may pray, and prayer may be an important part of your life, but you may also find it hard to be open about it. You feel it is private; perhaps you also feel it is inadequate, not good enough. This combination of not wanting to parade something that is intimate and not wanting to expose what is seen as a weakness means that, while many people may be able to talk about their belief in God, they recoil from speaking about their friendship with him. They also feel chary about opening the subject of how others pray. But a developing friendship with God is essential; it is at the very centre of all that we are about.

The community prays

Prayer is the work of the Church, the Body of Christ. As the Christian community we, ordinary men and women, are intimately caught up in the eternal relationship of love between Jesus and the Father in the Holy Spirit. That is the basis for our activity of praying. The worship that is part of the life of the Church comes first; it is one of the givens. During his lifetime, the prayer of Jesus was the open offering of himself to the will of the Father. The Church's offering continues this prayer and is caught up in the eternal relationship of Father and Son in the Holy Spirit. Each Christian has their place and their part in it.

This belief about prayer is expressed in what goes on in the local church on a Sunday and in the wonderfully varied ways in which men and women give their attention to God privately on their own and publicly with others.

Public prayer

There are several ways of sorting and labelling prayer. One is into 'public' and 'private'. Public prayer is the worship that the Christian community does together. The way it worships depends on the tradition of the local church as it meets to offer praise, thanks, penitence and prayer. Most follow some sort of pattern, often a formal liturgy as in the Eucharist.

For some newcomers and enquirers, as for some established church members, this joining in public worship may be their main, even their only, way of praying. In a week that is full of busyness, activity, pressure or strain, the church service stands as an oasis of refreshment when they can concentrate on their relationship with God.

Public prayer is the prayer of the community. It has an ongoing quality about it, its own life and validity. I take part in it, I also have my part in it. As a Christian, it is where I belong. It may also be the occasion when I say my own prayers, bring my own needs to God and offer my own gratitude. But the most important thing about public liturgy is that it is corporate; it expresses the truth that Christians belong together in the Body of Christ.

Private prayer

Praying on your own or with one or two other people is different from public worship. Most of the rest of this chapter is about the ways people pray as individuals and how they vary. The diagram on page 68 is designed as a help in looking at the different parts of ourselves that we bring into our praying. It is not complete, it does not answer every situation, but I offer it as a starting-point.

Words and systems

Some people have words as the main vehicle of their praying. The idea of saying prayers comes naturally to them, either praying aloud or simply forming words and phrases in their mind. They like books of prayers written by other people or collections that they have made for themselves. Sometimes they write their own prayers.

Such people like order and system in their relations with God. Daily prayers follow a pattern in which they feel at home; it is what they always do. Lists are helpful: lists of people, causes and institutions to pray for.

'Chatting with my friend God' is how one person described her prayer, going through the day and referring to him things that have happened, decisions that have to be made, problems and worries encountered. For her and for many others, prayer is a conversation either spoken or formed in the heart with a God who cares and listens and who occasionally is sensed to be replying.

Thoughts

Thinking about God, using your conscious mind to get in touch with him, to try to understand who he is or what he is about, is the natural way to pray for some people. The search for a meaning in life is all about how to explain things, how to make sense of it all. If these people use Bible study notes, for instance, they will be at home with the sort that end with 'questions for discussion'. They may well like to use a Bible that has references giving other passages to compare.

Faced with a problem, someone who prays in this way will spend time working it through with God. Their prayers often give space for planning, looking ahead to the day's events in their morning prayers, and to review at the end of the day.

Brian had been seriously ill. He nearly died. He told me afterwards that he had not been able to pray. He knew how ill he was. He recognized that he was facing the prospect of eternity and he found that he spent a lot of time in his illness trying to think what it would mean and where God came into it. He tried to face up to some part of his own death. Normally he prayed quite differently with a mixture of set prayers and a feeling of warmth towards God. He found it hard to

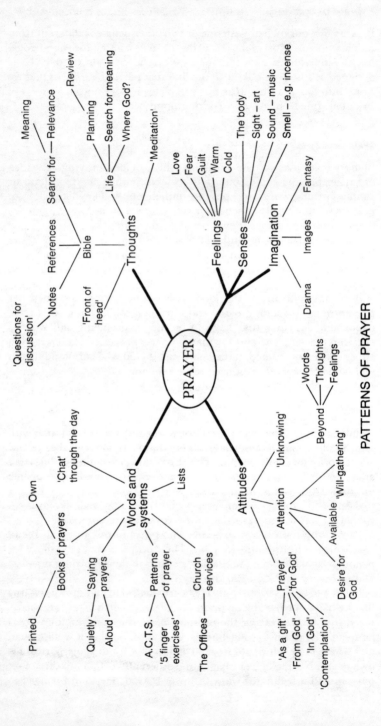

PATTERNS OF PRAYER

recognize that during his illness it was a case not of not being able to pray, but of learning to pray in a quite different way.

There are all the 'why?' questions that spring from the tragedies and meaningless disasters of personal and international life. How are people to come to terms with a loving God in the face of famines and injustice?

Feelings and images

This next section is about a very important part of being a person, which is to do with how we perceive, how we feel, and how we create. It looks at how an aspect of being human that is not to do with words and thinking leads into or expresses prayer. Part of this is about our bodies, our senses and our emotions. Part, also, is about our imagination and fantasies: I mean perceptions and faculties that are, to use rather technical words, 'affective' rather than 'intellectual' – praying in pictures, entering into stories, living out dramas, carried by music, expressing your relationship with God in song or in dance.

For people who use the Bible for prayer in this way, the gospels are not a quarry for texts to relate to other texts or for evidence to support this or that belief. They contain stories to be entered into. They present people to be met.

For thousands of years prayer has been sung or played on a musical instrument. If you appreciate Handel's *Messiah*, it is almost impossible to read the Bible texts on which it is based without hearing echoes of the music. I find that when in my prayers I want to express praise to God, it is often the tune of a well-known hymn of worship that means more than its words.

It can be the same for sight as it is for hearing. Things you see can move you to prayer, whether they are natural sights or works of art. It could be a sunset over the loch between the mountains, the soaring vaults of a great cathedral, or the colours and depth of an oil painting. Maybe it helps your prayer to have a lighted candle; perhaps you find it easier to pray with your eyes gently closed.

Then there is your imagination. It is about images, of course, but to use imagination in prayer is more than simply creating images. It is letting the non-rational, non-intellectual side of your personality have its proper place in your journey into God. People spend time happily fantasizing about all sorts of things: success at work, sexual encounters, what to do if they win the Pools. Not to mention the darker side of fantasy: the fears and anxieties that come to scare and disturb you, awake as well as dreaming. Fear of death or injury to someone you love in an accident. Even the simple fear that you didn't turn off the fire when you left home.

The prayer of images and imagination opens this side of a person to God. Rather than *thinking* about incidents in life or in the gospels, the person praying in this way *enters into them* in their imagination to experience the meaning for themselves.

Emotions play a large part in human life and they have their proper place in praying. For some people feelings are the heart of their prayer; for others just one aspect of it. But I think it is always worthwhile to notice how you feel, how you react. Feeling is more immediate than thinking. It often indicates what is deepest, perhaps where God is at work in the depths of your life. Notice feelings of warmth or distance, of love or shame or fear; being moved to prayer by anxiety about someone you love or by being afraid for yourself; enjoying a sense of comfort, reassurance and being in tune with God. In these and many other ways the affective side of our nature is either a way into prayer, a way of praying, or a way of experiencing the effect of prayer.

Attitudes

Feelings can often be a bridge leading into this fourth kind of prayer. Warmth, excitement, fear, anticipation, desire – all these, focused on God, can be a way towards the 'Prayer of Attitudes'. In this you direct your whole self towards God in love and openness. It may have an emotional content; you may have arrived by way of conversation with God, by way of thinking, or by way of imagination or feelings, but in this way of prayer you simply make yourself available to contemplate God as he is, and give him your attention, open to be aware of him, waiting in his presence.

It is a way of prayer that, because of its nature, is very hard to describe in words. Even pictures are little help. The title of a medieval book about it, *The Cloud of Unknowing*, emphasizes that it is not a prayer of the intellect. There is not much activity. You pray more by waiting, by being available. My image is of a she-cat hunting. She does not prowl dramatically about looking eager and menacing. She sits, at once alert and relaxed, and she listens. Her hunting consists largely of being aware of every sound in the long grass and discerning the distinct rustle made by a mouse or a vole.

When people talk about their experience of this 'contemplative' prayer, they make very tentative statements; they often use double negatives like 'I don't really know how to describe what happened in my prayer time today, but I know God was not absent'. You are involved in a prayer that takes place at a different level from thoughts and feelings. It is deeper and belongs to the most important part of your nature: your will. The choices you make and what you decide show what you really believe to be most important and valuable in your life. Reginald Somerset Ward, a notable Anglican spiritual director in the first half of this century, used to say 'The will is the voice of the soul'.

This way of praying more than any other illustrates the true purpose of prayer. It is *for God*. It points away from self, from my thoughts, feelings or concerns, and dwells entirely on God as he is. God is both the source of the prayer and its aim.

The body

People have bodies as well as souls, intelligence and feelings. Prayer is concerned with the physical in many different ways. Yoga has taught Western men and women the importance of posture, exercise and breathing in a search for well-being and a balanced life. They are important aspects of Christian prayer too.

Notice how your body is when you pray. Are you relaxed or tense, floppy or alert? Does it help to stand or kneel, to sit or to lie down? What does it mean for you to open your hands, palms upwards, and gently lift them to waist level . . . to shoulder level . . . to high above your head? What differences do you recognize when you are kneeling or sitting, standing or lying down as you pray? Movement and dance can also have their place in prayer.

Spiritual companionship

I would expect anyone reading these brief classifications to recognize something of their own experience in several, perhaps all, of them. I would also expect them to settle on one or two that are closest to their present way of praying. All are perfectly good and valid ways of praying for any Christian.

A Christian accompanying an enquirer should recognize how their friendship with God is growing and help it to develop in a way that is right for them. Sprituality varies and the enquirer's way may be quite different from the companion's. What suits one person can be quite improper for another.

Beware of expecting the other person to switch to your way of praying. Accept the truth that God has made people different and that he has given to each their own way to himself. Be prepared to listen for the ring of truth in other people's experience, however strange it may seem to you.

This work of accompanying demands an ability to listen, a gift of discernment, and a certain degree of background knowledge. It requires both enough confidence and enough humility. The confidence comes from having accepted that it is a proper part of the accompanying ministry to be a coach in spiritual matters and from having sufficient understanding of the basic principles of spirituality. It is also important to have backing and help from somebody else who is acting as *your* guide.

The humility comes from recognizing that the person you are accompanying has their own true spirituality and that your work is only to help them under God's guiding to grow into what he has planned for them to become.

John Westerhoff writes: 'The best guide on a spiritual journey is one who does not need to be helpful or needed, one who does not try to bear the responsibility of another life, but who can leave others in the hands of God – and get a good night's sleep. It is to take responsibility for one's own spiritual growth and to be with others as they do likewise.'

The givenness of prayer

Prayer is a dialogue; it is something that is a gift from God. He makes it possible for someone to pray. He is the inspiration. Without him there would be nothing. On the other hand, prayer is a human work. It requires effort on our part; it requires that we choose to put aside some time for it. We have to make ourselves available. We have continually to be recalling our wandering attention from all sorts of other thoughts, daydreams and interests to the business of seeking God.

The most common danger at all stages along the road to prayer seems to be the danger of over-worrying and guilt at the thought of being a failure. Prayer is a gift and our part in it is response to a gift.

In the four-way analysis of prayer on page 68 I was aware of a gap. The Charismatic Renewal sweeping through churches of all denominations speaks strongly of prayer as a gift from God, prayer as meeting a God who is Spirit, in human response to his call. This emphasis on the grace, the gift or, in religious technical language, the charism of praying should be recognized as a firm counter-balance to the common feeling that we need to work harder and harder to succeed in spirituality.

Variations and change

People who have prayed over a length of time, several months perhaps, several years certainly, will know that the 'temperature' of their praying varies considerably. There are times when it feels warm and meaningful to pray; God is real and near. It is quite easy. However, there are other times when all that disappears. Praying is a cold, dull and lonely activity. It becomes difficult to persuade yourself that there is anything in it. God seems totally absent, if he exists at all. Such variations are common to all praying Christians. 'I used to be able to pray. I used to enjoy it. But now I can't. It doesn't work for me any more.'

To put it simply, probably far too simply, there are two possible reasons for this experience of the emptiness of prayer. There is also another given, but, I find, very often mistaken. This usually false reason is the one that the person is most likely to offer themselves. It is that they are not trying hard enough; they think they ought to pray 'better', whatever that means, and they feel guilty about not doing so. This is a perfectly natural reaction, but in my experience it is usually wrong. It is an example of the danger of seeing prayer as a human activity only. It forgets the 'givenness'. What is far more likely is that the underlying cause is the regular dynamic of prayer. Like most human activities, it develops in phases. Periods of brightness are followed by duller periods. There are alternately times of encouragement and help, and times for developing our spiritual muscles. Dryness in prayer is a time for being faithful and staying with God; it is at this time that the Christian learns to live by hope and faith and love for that which is not seen.

The second reason concerns discernment, because the kind of boredom, anxiety and guilt that comes at one of these times of dryness can also be a sign that someone is trying to pray in the wrong way for them. It may be that they have set out to follow a model that does not suit them or it may be that they have changed within themselves and are growing into a new way of prayer.

The four ways of praying I described earlier in this chapter can be different stages in one person's spiritual development. It is not uncommon to begin with simple prayer in words, using a defined pattern of prayer. Later you may find the system too restricting and move into a more open, less wordy, approach to God through thinking, imagination, feelings or the will. The work of spiritual direction needs the sensitivity to notice the signs when someone ought to change and develop new ways of praying, or to support them as they come to terms with dryness.

Practicalities

I am aware that what I have written so far will not be appropriate for everybody. To develop a pattern of prayer along the lines I have suggested may well be easier for people who can find the space in their lives for privacy and who are able to devote time to it during their day. It is not that you cannot pray unless you have leisure; rather, it is that your pattern of prayer has to be appropriate to what your life's demands allow.

For instance, the demands on a mother of a baby or small children, or on someone caring for an invalid at home, may well mean that prayer is a matter of a few scattered moments of turning attention to God rather than keeping a daily period of time offered as God's time.

Busy people and people whose life and work ask a lot of them may see their prayer as being offered in the things they do. It is a prayer of action, doing a job well for God's sake, or consciously offering the care you show someone else in need as a kind of intercession.

The Practice of the Presence of God is a short book by a lay brother in a monastery whose work was in the kitchens. In it he describes a way of prayer that is real to very many people whose lives are full of activity and have little space. It is a way of carrying God with you all the time, working as if consciously in his presence, being aware of the spiritual within the everyday.

Pattern and rhythm

I have been helped by having what can be called a 'Rule of Life'. This is a way of describing the pattern of praying and other aspects of discipleship which are the basis of a person's spirituality. It could include how much time is given to prayer daily or weekly; the pattern of Bible reading and of church worship; the proportion of money given away; time for family or relaxation; and other aspects of self-discipline that are appropriate. A Rule of Life like this is something to be worked out in discussion with someone else. The pattern should be sensible, feasible, and not wildly beyond your ability! There is no point in setting such high standards that they can never be achieved. That simply compounds feelings of guilt. Although it is right for many people to work out some kind of regular pattern like this, there are others who find it quite wrong for them; what seems a rigid structure reduces the spontaneity of their relationship with God.

Praying with the Bible

The stories in the Bible are a central resource for someone who is trying to pray and grow in prayer. But it is a very hard book to find your way around. Anyone who is acting as a guide to a new Christian needs to be able to help them into a creative use of the Scriptures. This means, first of all, selection. Short passages, incidents, stories and sayings are the best material to work on in prayer. Slow repetitive reading to draw out meanings is often more fruitful than covering a lot of ground. So it is useful to have a system to select by. There are the Sunday readings; there are booklets of selections and notes published by the Bible Reading Fellowship, Scripture Union and many other organizations. These cover a range of approaches to the Bible and are written for a range of different ages, abilities and interests.

7

And Afterwards . . .?

One young woman writes:

> Easter morning at dawn I was baptized and confirmed. The service was very special, inasmuch as we went back in time to the early Church with all the richness and symbolism that it portrayed.
>
> The bishop, clergy and people gathered at dawn to celebrate the Easter liturgy, Service of Light, baptism and confirmation. Easter is a time when we vividly recall the death and resurrection of our Lord. I often refer to that morning as my wedding day with all the excitement and nerves of the occasion. I arrived just before 5.00 a.m. The chuch was in complete darkness and the air was full of expectation as if something wonderful was about to happen – and of course it was.
>
> Easter portrays just the start of our walk with our Lord. I was fully aware that my baptism and confirmation was just the beginning. I remember feeling very happy, a happiness that words cannot describe. I was floating like any bride on her wedding day and I knew he was happy too. I felt somehow he had given me so much more than I could ever give him in return. But he doesn't ask us to do that. All he wants is our love and I gave him that freely.
>
> A year has gone by since the all-important 'Yes, I do' and it has been a year of change and adjustment. I have been getting to know my Lord a little better and it takes time. My journey continues.

The events of the first Easter mark a new beginning in the relationship between God and his people. There is a new hope and a new purpose. The same is true for someone who is baptized or confirmed or has made an important act of recommitment. The celebration of either of these sacraments points to a new beginning. The preparation for the big event has been completed, but it needs to be recognized as preparation for a new life and a new work as a member of the Church. It has been a time of equipping a man or woman to be sent into the world to work for the coming of the rule of God in the affairs of individuals, of communities and of nations.

The Anglican Liturgical Consultation meeting in 1991 at Toronto concluded:

We see the catechumenal process affirming and celebrating the baptismal
identity of the whole community. As people participate in the process,
whether as enquirers, catechumens, candidates and initiates, or as sponsors, catechists and clergy, the *one baptism* by which all are incorporated in
the one body of Christ will be apprehended. . . . Through the lens of
baptism the people of God begin to see that lay ministry is important not
simply because it allows an interested few to exercise their individual
ministries, but because the ministry and mission of God in the church is
the responsibility of all the baptized community.

Baptism affirms the royal dignity of every Christian and their call and
empowering for active ministry within the mission of the church. . . . It
makes the church a sign and instrument of the new world that God is
establishing; it empowers Christians to strive for justice and peace within
society.

I hope it has been clear from the earlier parts of this book that the
purpose of the Adult Way to Faith is more than simply to help adults
to take part in the domestic events of the Church. It is all too easy for
clergy and lay leaders to think in terms of hands to do the jobs that
need doing in the life of the Christian community. 'Wonderful! Here
is Jim, who has just been confirmed. He's a motor mechanic, so let's
get him to service the parish minibus' – as if the purpose of the Gospel
was to make life easier for the group who believe! Far harder to grasp
and far more important for the Kingdom of God is a response rather
more like this: 'Wonderful! Here is Jim, who has just been confirmed.
He's a motor mechanic. What difference does his being confirmed
make to the way he does his job in the garage? What difference does
his being confirmed make to God's activity among the people who
manage and make up the staff at the garage? How can our church community help him and be associated with his ministry at work?'

Reflection leading to ministry

In the early Church the new Christians met with their bishop and other
leaders after their baptism at Easter until Pentecost to reflect on what
had happened to them in the baptismal water and in the breaking of
the bread. They were helped to enter into the meaning of the sacraments and to make that meaning their own. They were invited to say
for themselves, sometimes before the whole church, what difference
their preparation and their entry into the full life of the church made
to their lives.

The planning of the Adult Way to Faith in a parish must allow
plenty of time for this stage in the growth of today's new Christians.
The period before baptism or confirmation and the period after are
different. Certainly in the preparation time there should be work
together on what is likely to happen at baptism or confirmation and
how it will affect the way a person looks at life; but that is all looking
forward.

Once the event has happened, there is a change. Maggie has stood up before the whole church and made her profession of faith. The Church has celebrated with her a new beginning in the water of the font. The bishop has laid his hands on her head. Terry has invited members of his family who have scarcely ever attended church before to be with him at his confirmation; two friends from the dairy where he works came too. It means that there are new situations to be lived through and new questions to be asked. Once you have made that sort of public commitment, you are stuck with it and you have to see where it may lead you. Once you have been accepted and empowered by God and the Church, you have a new kind of life to live and explore.

It is a time for the kind of reflection that gives plenty of space for people to sense what is important for them, to notice and deepen their feelings and awareness – in fact, it is a time to be open to hearing what God has to say to the new Christians about what he has done for them and what he asks from them. In comparison with the time of preparation leading up to baptism or confirmation, it has been described as a time for poetry rather than for prose.

The group should help the candidates to enter into what took place at their baptism or confirmation. Invite them to tell the story of what happened to them, what it felt like, how they feel about it now. It is important to value their insights, their embarrassment, their pleasure or their sense of the ridiculous. Those who were their sponsors will also have their story to tell about how it felt to stand by their friends and present them.

For the Kingdom

During the preparation time the group has worked together on the subject of the Church's mission and ministry in the world. They spent a lot of time deepening their understanding of the Christian Gospel, its effect on their own lives, and its implications for the society in which they live. They became aware of God's gifts to them and developed some ability to speak about them.

The period after baptism and confirmation is to help them to build on these earlier experiences with the strength that has come to them through their baptism or confirmation so that they are able to fulfil their own part within the whole mission and ministry of the Church.

'Mission' is the overall word for the Church being sent into the world. Within that sending there are three main aspects of mission. They interlock with each other, and the boundaries between them are fluid, but there are also distinctions between them.

1. Evangelism

The Church is sent into the world to proclaim the Good News of the coming of the Kingdom of God, the Good News of the salvation of the world through the coming, the death and the resurrection of Jesus Christ. It is the work of the Church, which means the work of the men and women who make up the Body of Christ, to be witnesses to the Gospel and to help others into faith in Christ.

There is an interesting shift in meaning between some uses of the word 'evangelism' and some uses of the word 'evangelization'. I have noticed that among Anglicans and Protestants 'evangelism' often emphasizes the aspect of telling other people. To evangelize is to go out to others. A district that has been evangelized is a district in which missionaries have been active. The word 'evangelization' is more likely to be used by Catholics and tends to have a stronger content of conversion to it. For them, someone is evangelized who has not only heard the Gospel proclaimed, but has been moved to take it to heart. The process of evangelization is the process of presenting the Gospel and accompanying the hearer into faith.

The way to faith that we have worked through in this book responds to the challenge implicit in both these meanings. We are dealing with people to whom the Church has in one way or another announced the Good News. They are also people who through the accompanied journey into faith have been helped to open their hearts to that Good News and be changed by it.

In this period after their 'Easter', the purpose of the group is to work with them and see how the new Christians are to live out the calling to go and tell others. The story of Mary Magdalen at the tomb in St John's gospel gives a picture of this. Notice her movement away from being primarily a learner, someone who is dependent, towards being a person who is liberated to give to others and who, moreover, recognizes that she has been given authority to do so.

The style of the group during the period of learning and growing and during the final preparation helped the members to grow in confidence in speaking as well as listening. All the people taking part had the opportunity to develop confidence in sharing faith with one another. So it should not be too great a shock for the newly baptized or confirmed member of the Church to be asked to tell their story and talk about what they believe to another person. The preparation for Christian initiation is a preparation for sharing in evangelism as one aspect of the whole work of the Church.

2. *Service*

At the height of the Christian Stewardship movement, when there was something like a blueprint for Stewardship Campaigns for parishes to follow, the section on 'Time and Talents' usually came after the big drive on money. As often as not, it fell flat on its face. In the same way that the 'money part' was generally seen as designed to provide cash for the church (however much that image failed to do justice to the underlying truths about people and their responsibility for God's gifts), so 'Time and Talents' came to be seen as asking what skills church people had to offer for the work of the congregation and the parish. Very rarely was the question asked 'How are you to offer the time and the talents which God has given you in your *daily work?*'

Many years ago I was chaplain in a television company, since closed down. Two of the senior technicians had been moved by Christian Stewardship in their different churches. They recognized that the talents they had to offer God were their skills as, respectively, a sound supervisor and an engineer. Fired by their enthusiasm, we got together a working group which assembled a complete volunteer studio crew which was willing to work for the church at weekends when the studio was not in use. The company itself agreed to the free use of the studio. The trouble was that when we offered this remarkable facility to the church authorities, they had no idea how to use it.

Once lay people in the Church begin to play their full part in the formation of other lay Christians, then interest begins to focus more and more on the relationship between their faith and that area of their lives which takes up the working day and provides the money for them to buy the things they need. Work matters to men and women. Facing unemployment matters. Caring for a home and family matters. Living alone and coping with increasing disability matter. These are the situations where faith has to be worked out in practice. Of course people will have worked on these things during the time of preparation; but in this period of reflection leading to ministry they are right in the forefront.

The Church is a community called to serve the needs of the poor. St John's picture of Jesus washing the feet of his disciples at the Last Supper fills out the description of his calling in St Luke's story when he read from the book of Isaiah at the Nazareth synagogue service. All Christians are asked for generous giving of time and effort for other people, as well as proper giving of money. Often it is the newer members of the church who give an example to those of longer standing. During this time of reflection the group should consider what local or more distant needs are presented to the church and what part the new Christians are to play in meeting those needs. Their answers may challenge the rest of the congregation to a reawakening.

3. Body building

There is a real need for continuing growth and development of the Christian community if it is to be able to fulfil this commission to evangelize and to serve. New Christians and old alike need the chance to learn and to mature. They need the support and encouragement of one another and of their leaders, clergy and others.

So an element in the reflection leading to ministry is to see what part it is right for the new members to play within the life of the local church. There are all the possible ministries in Sunday services; there may be opportunities for taking part in one of the organizations of the parish; there are openings for practical work with people in their homes or around the church buildings.

It may be that within a fairly short time it is right to invite a new Christian to act as sponsor to someone who is beginning their journey of faith. But this should not be too soon.

Closing down

Obviously the Adult Way to Faith in one sense never ends in this life. As human beings we are continually changing and regularly making new decisions. It is the same with the Christian life. If you are not open to growth and movement, you are dead. So one of the gifts that I believe this Way has to offer the Church is its emphasis on the importance of a conversion which is lifelong and on the duty of Christians to accompany one another along this journey.

You can't, or at least most people shouldn't, stay a beginner for ever. There comes a time when the initial stage of the journey is over and a new sort of life as a firmly belonging Christian takes over. Discipleship never closes down. As a companion of Jesus Christ you are always a learner; but in time you are also invited to become an apostle, someone who is sent out as part of his or her mission to the world. The period of reflection leading to ministry is about this transition.

When should the groups end? How should they finish? What continuing care should be available for new Christians? These are all very important questions, but there are no clear-cut, hard and fast answers.

The Roman Catholic bishops of the USA, in their introduction to the Rite of Christian Initiation of Adults, suggest that the preparation for baptism should last at least a full year, preferably 15 months, and that there should be at least monthly meetings for new Christians over the year following their baptism to support them in their 'deeper Christian formation and incorporation into the full life of the Christian community'.

Individual needs will vary, and so will different groups. New Christians should find the support they need from those who have accompanied them till now, but the clergy and other leaders should make sure that this is in fact happening.

Groups, especially groups that have the kind of strong fellowship that comes through following this Way together, develop a strong life of their own. The love and mutual support that characterize them mean that members often find it hard to stop meeting. People need help in dealing with the kind of bereavement that closure means. Some of the best parties I have been to have been the ones to mark the end of regular group sessions!

Discernment is needed to find the right choices in particular situations. It may be right for a group that began as a preparation group for certain people to continue as, say, a house group within the life of the church. Or it may be better for the people in it to divide, to join existing groups, or help in the formation of new ones. The fellowship that grew over the months is not lost; friendships built along the journey of faith have a lasting quality.

Group work

Detailed suggestions for your own place and the actual men and women concerned should ideally grow naturally out of the individual and group experiences of the past months. The journey of the Adult Way to Faith that we have followed in this book is only the first part of a lifelong pilgrimage in Christ and within the fellowship of his body, the Church. I trust that it will lead all who follow into ever deeper awareness of his love and deeper commitment to his service.

However, it may help to point to a few areas that the group can work on during this time after the baptism or confirmation of those who have been accompanied during their preparation.

1. Reflection

Spend plenty of time simply recalling what has happened. Let everyone say for themselves what it was like to be baptized or confirmed, or to be there as a friend or sponsor; what it is like to receive holy communion. Give space to talk about awarenesses, perceptions and feelings of all sorts.

Consider what the event means to the people who took part, what effect it has had on them, what difference it has made. Whether or not it was at the Easter season, see what the dying and rising with Christ means for the candidates. Help them to 'make it their own' and find appropriate ways of living it out.

The gospels for Easter Day and the following Sundays provide a good resource for this kind of exploration.

2. Ministry

Look together at what practical changes follow from this reflection. Areas to notice include choices and relationships at home and at work; church life, both in its worship and in its social and practical life; involvement in issues of peace and justice and in the service of those in need locally and elsewhere; spirituality and the development of each person's relationship with God and its expression in life.

3. Church

Ask what difference the work of the past months and in particular the baptism and confirmation of the candidates has made or should make to the life of the local church. What has the group to offer to the wider congregation? How should they make that offer known?

Consider whether it would be right for those newly baptized and confirmed to speak about their journey and their experiences at one of the main Sunday services.

4. Closure

Spend plenty of time looking at the ending of the life and work of the group. Acknowledge the feelings the members have about not meeting regularly in the future. Fix a clear timetable for these final meetings. If it seems appropriate, organize a party to celebrate the beginning of a new stage in the journey.

Make suitable arrangements for the continuing accompaniment of the new members over the months to come.

8

Celebrating the Journey: The Rites

This chapter gives three sets of suggestions for services to mark the main stages on the Adult Way to Faith. There are models to be found in the Anglican Communion, as well as in the Roman Catholic Rite of Christian Initiation of Adults.

But parishes and churches should design liturgies that suit the actual situation in the local church. Sometimes these have been very simple indeed. For instance, the Welcome might consist of a short introduction by the vicar or minister, followed by the candidates being invited to come forward with their sponsors to be introduced to the congregation, greeted with a Right Hand of Fellowship, and commended for God's blessing in prayer. Others have used or adapted the Roman Rite or the American Episcopalian order with varying degrees of freedom.

The six outlines for the Service of Welcome and God's Call that follow are offered as examples to choose from. John Hill is a priest in the Anglican Church of Canada who works in a parish in Toronto. For the Service of Welcome (1) and God's Call (1) I have made some adjustments to the liturgies that he offers in his book, *Making Disciples*. For the second pair of examples I have drawn heavily on the work of two churches, St Thomas's, Holtspur, in Beaconsfield, and St Martin-in-the-Fields, London, to share something of the experience of Anglican parishes in England. The third pair of services is taken with a few amendments from *Follow Me*, the confirmation course produced by the Additional Curates Society.

There are two ways in which these examples can be used. They can be seen as a quarry from which ideas or whole sections may be taken by people designing liturgies for their own churches. Or they may be used whole as they stand, in which case parishes buying this book are free to photocopy pages from it for their own local use in worship.

Baptized and unbaptized

Most of the people who follow the Adult Way to Faith as enquirers will be candidates for confirmation. They will usually have been christened as babies. However, the proportion of those who are not baptized is going to increase as the 1990s unfold into the next century. Indeed, there is already a significant number in adult preparation classes.

The difference between candidates for baptism and candidates for confirmation needs to be recognized in the design and celebration of the liturgies marking stages along the way. In baptism, a person has joined the Church. He or she is already a member. The words of the service for someone preparing for confirmation must give full value to this.

The Service of Welcome

What for?

The purpose of the service is to mark the start of a person's committed journey, the first signs of their Christian faith, and their joining a group to begin a course that may lead to baptism, confirmation or the reaffirmation of their baptismal vows.

It expresses the congregation's welcome to enquirers or new members. The church hears the request that an enquirer makes and accepts it. The enquirer is given a sign of their belonging, either the sign of the cross, a copy of the New Testament or the gospels, or perhaps a handshake. There is prayer for them. Sponsors may be commissioned for their ministry with the enquirers.

When and where

In a parish Eucharist the Welcome takes place either at the very beginning of the service, which can be a sign of enquirers being welcomed to the church as it learns from the Ministry of the Word, or after the sermon, which gives the opportunity for preaching about the event and its importance before it happens.

In a church where a parish Eucharist is not the tradition, a Family Service or Morning or Evening Prayer should be built round the theme of welcoming new people to the community.

It is best if there is actual movement of people through the building, bringing the new members in from outside the church, from the porch or from the back of the church to the front, introducing them to the congregation and then accepting them into their place as part of the community.

Their sponsors should stand and move with the enquirers throughout the service.

In churches with sound amplification, care should be taken that the different times of dialogue are heard by the whole church.

Suitable music should be chosen for appropriate points in the rite.

Celebrations of God's Call

What for?

This service, against the background of a belief in a God who chooses and calls his people, makes formal and celebrates the Church's invitation and the enquirer's readiness for baptism, confirmation or the reaffirmation of baptismal vows. It expresses the process of discernment that has already taken place among the people responsible, and affirms the congregation's support.

Where the confirmation is not to take place in the candidates' church, this rite can be adapted to commend them for confirmation at another centre.

When?

In the parish Eucharist, the rite takes place after the sermon.

It may form the theme for a Family Service, Morning or Evening Prayer in churches where the Eucharist is not the main Sunday service.

Other celebrations of the journey

Some parishes follow the pattern of the early Church and celebrate other occasions along the journey. These may include 'The Giving of the Creed' and 'The Giving of the Lord's Prayer'. In Lent there are the powerful liturgies of self-examination, penitence and special prayer, which form part of the final preparation of candidates for baptism or confirmation at Easter. Forms of service for these can be found in books listed in Chapter 9.

Baptism, Confirmation and Eucharist

The liturgy for the baptism of adults with confirmation and the Eucharist is to be found in the Alternative Service Book. *Lent, Holy Week and Easter* provides an order for the Easter Vigil. Both these can be developed and adapted within the limits given so that the celebration makes a fitting climax to the journey of initiation that the candidates have followed.

Reaffirmation

People who have already been baptized and confirmed when much younger and have come by the Way to a renewed adult faith have the opportunity to celebrate the renewal of baptismal vows at the same service as their companions are confirmed. Again, this is found in the Alternative Service Book and should be celebrated with imagination and relevance to the people taking part.

Without in any sense making the event a 're-baptism', it is possible to use water as a sign in this renewal. Either the person may be sprinkled or they may use water themselves.

Anointing with oil is an ancient sign used by the early Church at different points along the enquirer's journey. The scented Oil of Chrism in particular has its use with those who are newly baptized and those who are renewing their vows.

Worksheet 8A:
Planning the Service of Welcome

Preparation

Ensure that the people who need to be are invited to the meeting or kept informed of decisions. These may include, among others, the clergy, the organist, servers, churchwardens, group leaders and sponsors.

Task

1. Decide the order of service, choosing from the following examples or designing your own. Arrange photocopying if necessary.
2. Work out the movements of people in the service.
3. Choose the music.
4. Decide if you need a rehearsal for sponsors and make arrangements accordingly.

Service of Welcome (1)

Presentation

The enquirers may be brought by the sponsors to the entrance of the church. After the opening greeting, the president, with other members of the congregation, goes out to greet them and encourages the others to remember their own journey in faith.

The president then invites the sponsor to speak on behalf of the enquirer. The sponsor says:
I present *N* who wishes to follow the way of Christ.

The president asks of the enquirer:
What do you seek?

Answer **Knowledge of Christ.** (*Or a personal reply, prepared in advance.*)

The president replies as follows or in similar words adapted to the answer:
God gives the light of life to everyone who comes into the world, so that those who seek the Lord may truly find him and live in his joy for ever. You have followed that light; and the way to that joy lies before you.

You have come to seek the face of the Lord. Do you intend to share in the Church's worship of God and service to the poor and receive guidance in the way of Christ?

Answer **I do.**

Are you ready to open your ears to hear the word of God and your heart to receive the Good News of our Lord Jesus Christ?

Answer **I am.**

To the sponsors and the congregation the president says:
Dear friends in Christ, will you support *N* and *N* by prayer and by example and help them to grow in the knowledge and love of God and of God's Son, Jesus Christ our Lord?

Answer **We will.**

Thanksgiving and Signing

The president prays for the enquirers, saying:
God of steadfast love, on behalf of our friends *N* and *N* we offer thanks and praise to you for the experience of your guiding presence which has brought them to this day.

Help us to serve them faithfully with the kindness you have shown us and to accept with joy all the gifts they bring. Together may we offer ourselves in your service, seeking your Kingdom and the honour of your holy name; through Jesus Christ our Lord. **Amen.**

The president marks each enquirer with the sign of the cross, saying:
N, accept the sign of the cross of Christ; be assured of his great love
for you and learn to know and follow him.
The president then says to the enquirers:
Come now and share with us in hearing the word of the Lord.
*The president leads the people into the church, giving the enquirers their place
among the people. A suitable hymn may be sung during this procession. The service
continues with the Collect for the Day and the Ministry of the Word.*

Handing on the Gospel

*Before the intercessions, a Bible or New Testament may be presented to the
enquirers with these or similar words:*
Receive the good news; take hold on eternal life. May you find in
Jesus Christ a true friend.

The Intercessions

*The prayers and thanksgivings should include prayer for those newly welcomed
and their sponsors.*
*If a litany form is used, parts of the following may be included and adapted
as appropriate:*
Leader In peace let us pray to the Lord, saying 'Lord, have mercy'.
For N and N that they may be confirmed in their desire to seek God
and given grace to persevere, let us pray to the Lord.

Lord, have mercy.

Leader That the flame of faith and hope and love may be kindled in
their heart as they learn the story of our salvation, let us pray to the
Lord.

Lord, have mercy.

Leader That they may know the grace of our Lord Jesus Christ and
may turn to him in repentance and faith, let us pray to the Lord.

Lord, have mercy.

Leader That the wounds of sin may be healed in them and that they
may be strengthened to know God's will and to do it with joy, let
us pray to the Lord.

Lord, have mercy.

Leader That their vision may be enlarged to encompass all the pro-
mised joys of God's Kingdom, let us pray to the Lord.

Lord, have mercy.

Leader That in finding light and life they may become signs of God's grace and promise to us and to others, let us pray to the Lord.

Lord, have mercy.

Leader That we may be faithful in our care for them and that they may be established in the fellowship of the Holy Spirit, let us pray to the Lord.

Lord, have mercy.

Leader That those who teach the way of Christ may impart all the riches of God's holy word, let us pray to the Lord.

Lord, have mercy.

The intercessions may close with the following:
Eternal God,
You are the light of the minds that know you,
the joy of hearts that love you,
and the strength of wills that serve you.
Grant us so to know you that we may truly love you;
and so to love you that we may fully serve you,
for in serving you is perfect freedom
through Jesus Christ our Lord. **Amen.**

Service of Welcome (2)

After the sermon the congregation stands.

President The Lord be with you.

Congregation **And also with you.**

President The life of faith in Jesus Christ is a journey of discovery. Today we rejoice with *N* and *N* as they set out on a new stage in that journey, which they will share with their sponsors who have come from among us to accompany them. We pray for them and for ourselves that we may all be worthy of our calling:

Almighty God, by whose grace alone we are accepted and called to your service; strengthen us by your Holy Spirit and make us worthy of our calling; through Jesus Christ our Lord. Amen.

The president then directs that the candidates should come forward and a hymn is sung.

EITHER

President My brothers and sisters in Christ, do you want to enter into the Christian Way of Life?

OR

Do you accept your life in Christ through baptism?

Candidate **Yes, I do.**

OR

President What do you seek?

Candidate (*A personal reply is given.*)

President God enlightens everyone who comes into the world. You have followed his light. Now the way opens before you, inviting you to make a new beginning. You are called to walk by the light of Christ and to trust in his wisdom. This is the way of faith on which Christ will lovingly guide you. Are you ready to enter on this path?

Candidate **I am.**

Each candidate kneels to receive a blessing and/or is signed with the cross. Their sponsor is asked:

President Will you accompany *N*, supporting and strengthening him/her by your friendship, love and prayers?

Sponsor **I will.**

When all the candidates have been received, the whole congregation is asked:

President As members of this church will you all try to befriend these disciples of the Lord, to get to know them, to welcome them and to uphold them by your prayers?

All **Yes, we will.**

President We pray now for these our brothers and sisters who have been called to follow our Lord Jesus Christ, that the faith which God has implanted in their hearts may grow to a rich harvest.

(*Silence.*)

Father, all-powerful and ever-living God, fountain of light and truth, source of eternal love, hear our prayers for your servants. Cleanse them of sin, make them holy, give them true knowledge, firm hope and sound faith; so that their hearts will be prepared for the grace of your sacraments. We ask this in the name of Jesus Christ our Lord. Amen.

President May the Lord God bless you, protect you from all evil, guide you in his way and fulfil your desires.

All **Amen.**

The Eucharist continues with The Peace.

Service of Welcome (3)

Introduction

President Our friends have been discovering the joy of the Gospel of Christ through study and prayer and fellowship. They come today to ask to be enrolled as candidates for the sacrament of confirmation. It gives us great joy to welcome them and support them as they take this step in faith.

Questions to the candidates

President God enlightens everyone who comes into the world. You have followed his light. Now the way of Christ opens before you, inviting you to make a new beginning. You are called to walk by the light of Christ and to trust his wisdom. He asks you to submit yourself to him more and more, and to believe in him with all your heart. This is the pilgrimage of faith, in which Christ will lovingly guide you to eternal life. Are you ready to enter upon this path today?

Candidates **I am.**

President Do you desire the new life that Jesus Christ offers you, through the gift of his Holy Spirit?

Candidates **Yes, I do.**

President Do you reject from your life everything contrary to the Gospel; all resentment, all jealousy, all selfishness, all sinful habits?

Candidates **Yes, I do.**

President Do you believe that the new life of the Spirit was chosen for you when you were baptized?

Candidates **Yes, I do.**

President Do you now, from your own heart, desire to endorse that choice once made for you and begin preparation for the sacrament of confirmation?

Candidates **Yes, I do.**

President May the Lord bless you, protect you from evil and guide you in his way.

Question to the sponsors

President Sponsors are called to accompany our brothers and sisters in
their journey forwards in faith and to strengthen them by their
friendship, love and prayers.

Sponsors, do you undertake to encourage your friends by your
intercession, example and help, and so lead them forward into the
new life they have freely chosen?

Sponsors **Yes, I do.**

Question to the congregation

President Will you welcome these candidates, get to know them more
deeply and uphold them with your prayers?

All **We will.**

The signing and anointing

*The candidates kneel. The president anoints each one with the oil of catechumens,
saying*:

We anoint you with the oil of salvation in the name of Christ our
saviour. By this sign of his love Christ will be your strength. Learn
to know and follow him.

Giving of the Gospel

*Each candidate, still kneeling, is presented with a copy of the gospels by the presi-
dent or reader, saying*:

Receive the Gospel, the Good News of Jesus Christ, the Son of God.

Concluding prayer

President Father of love and mercy, we thank you in the name of our
brothers and sisters who have experienced your guiding presence in
their lives. Today, in the presence of your family they are answering
your call to faith. Lead them by your Holy Spirit into the joys you
have prepared for them. May your whole Church advance in its
journey of faith, and come to find with all your saints the fullness
of eternal life. We ask this through Jesus Christ our Lord.

All **Amen.**

The service continues with The Peace.

Worksheet 8B:
Planning the Celebration of God's Call

1. Discernment

At an appropriate review session clergy and lay leaders should pray for and talk about the people who are in preparation for baptism and confirmation.

Notice how each feels about the readiness or otherwise of the candidates to be presented for initiation.

Spend time discussing people about whom there are questions. Decide how to approach them before coming to final conclusions.

Try to be clear about the different responsibilities of the individual candidates concerned, the leaders of the groups and the parish clergy in this discernment.

2. Service preparation

(a) Decide who are the appropriate people to be involved in preparation and who has to be kept informed.

(b) Decide on the form of service and arrange photocopying if necessary.

(c) Decide on the method of presentation of the candidates. Is it to be formal or informal?

(d) Decide on what movements are to take place and what symbols are to be used.

God's Call (1)

After the sermon the sponsors lead the candidates forward and present them to the president in the following or similar words:

I present to you *N* and *N*, who have been strengthened by God's grace and the prayers of this congregation and ask that they be accepted as candidates for baptism [or confirmation].

The president asks the sponsors:

Have they been regular in attending the worship of God and in receiving instruction?

Answer (A personal reply is given.)

Are they seeking by prayer, study and example to pattern their lives in accordance with the Gospel?

Answer (A personal reply is given.)

The president may ask for commendation of the candidates from members of the congregation. He then asks the candidates:

Do you desire to be baptized [confirmed]?

Answer **I do.**

The president may then ask the congregation:

Brothers and sisters, will you open your hearts to these people whom God is calling to be changed into the likeness of his own Son?

People **We will.**

President Will you watch and pray with them as they pass over from death to life through the waters of baptism?

People **We will.**

The president then turns to the candidates and, taking each one by the hand, says:

In the name of God and with the consent of this congregation I accept you as a candidate for holy baptism [or confirmation].
The president may lay a hand on the head of each, saying:
May almighty God who tests the motives of our hearts give you courage to obey the call of Christ. May you be strengthened by God's Spirit to stand against the powers of evil, and to persevere in every trial of your faith; and the blessing of God, Father, the Son and Holy Spirit be upon you now and for ever. **Amen.**
All may then return to their places.

The prayers

If a litany form is used, parts of the following may be included and adapted as appropriate:

Leader In peace let us pray to the Lord, saying 'Lord, have mercy'. For *N* and *N*, that they may be freed from the yoke of Satan and bear the gentle yoke of Christ, let us pray to the Lord.

Lord, have mercy.

Leader That in coming to a knowledge of their sin against God and against their neighbours they may truly repent and be truly healed, let us pray to the Lord.

Lord, have mercy.

Leader That they may be protected from all worldly illusions and given courage to accept the challenge of the Christian way, let us pray to the Lord.

Lord, have mercy.

Leader That being established in God's love, they may know their worth and become good stewards of the gift of life, let us pray to the Lord.

Lord, have mercy.

Leader That being delivered from all selfishness their lives may be enriched with love for others, let us pray to the Lord.

Lord, have mercy.

Leader That as God reveals his purpose in their lives, their daily occupations may become a pleasing sacrifice, let us pray to the Lord.

Lord, have mercy.

Leader That we may all prepare [during this season of Lent] with eager expectation for the paschal celebration, let us pray to the Lord.

Lord, have mercy.

The leader may conclude the prayers with the following:
Gracious Father, grant that all who are baptized into Jesus Christ your Son may be cleansed from every evil, commit their lives to you, and share in the eternal priesthood of Christ our Lord; for to him, to you and to the Holy Spirit belong all glory and blessing, now and for ever. Amen.

God's Call (2)

After the sermon the congregation stands.
President The Lord be with you.

Congregation **And also with you.**

A group leader says:
Our friends are completing their time of preparation. They have
been strengthened by God's grace and supported by this community's example and prayers. They come today to ask that they may
soon be allowed to enter into the full sacramental life of the Church.

President The life of faith in Jesus Christ is a journey of discovery. At
the Service of Welcome we rejoiced with *N* and *N* and supported
them with our prayers as they entered a new stage on their journey.
Today we celebrate with them as they commit themselves to accept
their responsibility within the priesthood of all believers and
approach [baptism and] confirmation. We pray for them, their
sponsors and ourselves that we may all be worthy of our calling.
Almighty God, by whose grace alone we are accepted and called to
your service: strengthen us by your Holy Spirit and make us worthy
of our calling; through Jesus Christ our Lord. Amen.
The president then invites the candidates and sponsors to come forward.

President These people have asked to be admitted into the full sacramental life of the Church. For a long time they have heard the word
of Christ and have been trying to live in his way. Those who know
them judge them to be sincere in their desire. I now ask the sponsors
to affirm their support.
You have accompanied *N* on his/her journey. Do you believe that
he/she is ready to make this commitment?

Sponsor (*A personal reply is given.*)

President Are you willing to renew [to make] your baptism commitment in Christ?

Candidate **I am.**

President Do you agree that these candidates should go forward for
[baptism and] confirmation?

Congregation **We do.**

President (*to each candidate*)
N, you have been chosen and called to enter into the fullness of the
Christian mysteries.

Candidate **Thanks be to God.**

President (addressing the candidates)

Now it is your duty and ours to ask the help of God. He is always faithful to those he calls.

(addressing the sponsors)

These people have been entrusted to you in the Lord. By your loving care and example, go on helping them and praying for them as they look forward to receiving the sacraments of salvation.

May the Lord bless you, protect you from all evil and guide you in his way.

A short litany is said.

Leader In peace let us pray to the Lord, saying 'Lord, have mercy'.

For these candidates, that they may remember with thanksgiving this day on which they were chosen, let us pray to the Lord.

Lord, have mercy.

Leader For the period of preparation before their confirmation, that it may be a time of renewal and hopefulness, let us pray to the Lord.

Lord, have mercy.

Leader For all those who accompany seekers after faith and for those who preach and teach, that they may be given discernment and strength, let us pray to the Lord.

Lord, have mercy.

Leader For the families and friends of the candidates, that they may be a source of encouragement and understanding, let us pray to the Lord.

Lord, have mercy.

Leader For this congregation, that with the candidates we too may enter into this period of renewal and may grow in love, let us pray to the Lord.

Lord, have mercy.

Leader For our Bishop, *N*, and for all the church, let us pray to the Lord.

Lord, have mercy.

The Eucharist continues at The Peace.

God's Call (3)

The introduction

President For all God's people, this holy season is a time for renewal in prayer and discipleship, as we journey together towards Holy Week and Easter, in the strength of the Holy Spirit.

For our confirmation candidates in particular, today marks a new stage in their personal pilgrimage of faith. For several months they have been exploring the Good News of Jesus Christ and discovering the Christian way. Today they ask that they may begin to prepare for the celebration of the holy sacraments, assured of our support and our prayers.

The president calls forward the candidates by name, who take their places at the front, the sponsors standing behind.

Question to the sponsors

President Our brothers and sisters have asked to be admitted into the full sacramental life of the Church. For some time you have been encouraging and supporting them in their journey of faith. Do you consider our friends ready to prepare for this?

Sponsors **We do.**

The congregation now stands.

Question to the congregation

President From the outset of their spiritual journey, our friends have depended on the prayers and encouragement of all God's family at [name of church]. Will you help them in this season of grace to grow in prayer and discipleship, through your example, your intercessions and your words of support?

All **We will.**

Question to the candidates

President Dear friends, your sponsors and the entire Christian family here at [name of church] are behind you in your desire to follow Christ more closely. In the name of our Saviour, we invite you now to prepare to enter into the fullness of the Christian life.

Do you wish to dedicate these holy days to Christ, to prepare carefully to enter into the greatest mysteries of the crucified and risen Lord?

Candidates **We do.**

The candidates kneel.

The President gives each one a copy of the Revised Catechism or some other suitable book to help them in their study of the sacraments. Going along the line, the priest says to each candidate in turn:

You have been chosen and called to enter into the fullness of the Christian life.

Candidates **Thanks be to God.**

The candidates kneeling, all pray together:

God our Father, creator of the human race, you make all things new in your Son Jesus Christ, bless these your servants and make them truly your children.

Guard them all their lives,

by the power of the Holy Spirit may they know the gift of eternal life.

We ask this through Jesus Christ our Lord. Amen.

The candidates stand.

President Candidates, you have been chosen by God and called to join all followers of Jesus Christ in our pilgrimage to glory. May Christ be your way, your truth and your life. We look forward soon to welcoming you with joy into the fellowship of the Eucharist.

The service continues with The Peace.

9

Resources

Networks

In the United Kingdom, the Catechumenate Network provides an opportunity for Anglicans and others to meet and learn from one another at regular training days and conferences. It also publishes a newsletter several times a year. Its address is Whittonedge, Whittonditch Road, Ramsbury, Wiltshire SN8 2PX.

The Roman Catholic Church in England and Wales has its RCIA National Co-ordinator at the General Secretariat, 39 Ecclestone Square, London SW1.

The European Conference on the Adult Catechumenate meets every two years to exchange information and develop the work of the catechumenate. The secretariat is provided by the French Service National du Catéchuménat, 4 avenue Vavin, 75006 Paris.

In the USA the North American Forum on the Catechumenate offers comprehensive training institutes for various aspects of the catechumenate and publishes a regular journal. The address is 5510 Columbia Pike, Suite 310, Arlington, VA 22204. The Office of Evangelism Ministries of the Episcopal Church is based at the Episcopal Church Center, 815 Second Avenue, New York, NY 10017.

Books

On the process

The Rite of Christian Initiation of Adults: A Study Book (St Thomas More Centre, London, 1988) gives the official Roman Catholic text and provides commentaries on its use.

The Book of Occasional Services: Second Edition (The Church Hymnal Corporation, New York, 1988) contains official Anglican services and directions for the catechumenate, produced by the Episcopal Church's Standing Liturgical Commission.

The Catechumenal Process (Office of Evangelism Ministries, The Episcopal Church) (The Church Hymnal Corporation, New York,

1990) outlines the heart of the process for today's Church.

John W. B. Hill, *Making Disciples: Serving Those who are Entering the Christian Life* (The Hoskin Group, Toronto, 1991) offers an 'Order for Catechesis', outlining a pastoral ministry to use with people entering the Christian faith and liturgies to celebrate their conversion journey.

Thomas H. Morris, *The RCIA: Transforming the Church: A Resource for Pastoral Implementation* (Paulist Press, New York, 1989) is by the Director of the North American Forum. It is written from a base of experience in the catechumenate and of accompanying people into Christian faith and committed ministry in the world.

Malcolm Grundy, *Evangelization Through the Adult Catechumenate* (Grove Books, Nottingham, 1991) is a short handbook on the Adult Way to Faith, recommended as an introduction for lay people in the parish.

Peter Ball, *Adult Believing* (Mowbray, London and Oxford, 1988) is an introduction for parish clergy and lay people to the ideas and practice of the catechumenate.

James B. Dunning, *New Wine, New Wineskins* (Sadlier, New York, 1981) is one of the early American books giving a clear and attractive introduction to the process.

Background

William Abraham, *The Logic of Evangelism* (Hodder & Stoughton, London, 1989) offers creative and critical insights into the theory and practice of evangelism today, giving full weight to the process of conversion and personal journey.

How Faith Grows: Faith Development and Christian Education (National Society/Church House Publishing, London, 1991) relates the insights of such writers as James W. Fowler to the work of churches and schools. (James Fowler is the author of *Stages of Faith* and *Becoming Adult, Becoming Christian*.)

Adult Christian education

Anton Baumohl, *Making Adult Disciples* (Scripture Union, London, 1984) makes full use of modern adult education experience in a useful guide for the local church.

Patrick Purnell (ed.), *To be a People of Hope* (Collins, London, 1987) is not only a book about adult education, but an aid in enabling the process to happen.

Christian Basics (Church Pastoral Aid Society, Athena Drive, Warwick CV34 6NG) is a training kit of 24 sessions from which to create a local programme for new enquirers and those preparing for baptism and confirmation. It includes loose-leaf material for photocopying and two videos.

Follow Me (Additional Curates Society, 264a Washwood Heath

Road, Birmingham B8 2XS) is a pack of confirmation preparation
material in three sections for children, teenagers and adults. It
includes candidates' workbooks, leaders' notes and specimen liturgies
for various stages of the process.